Education, Class Language and Ideology

Education, Class Language and Ideology

Noëlle Bisseret
Centre National de la Recherche Scientifique

ROUTLEDGE & KEGAN PAUL
London, Boston and Henley

First published in 1979
by Routledge & Kegan Paul Ltd
39 Store Street, London WC1E 7DD,
Broadway House, Newtown Road,
Henley-on-Thames, Oxon RG9 1EN and
9 Park Street, Boston, Mass. 02108, USA
Set in Press Roman by
Hope Services, Abingdon
and printed in Great Britain by
Lowe & Brydone Ltd
Thetford, Norfolk
© Noëlle Bisseret 1979

British Library Cataloguing in Publication Data

Bisseret, Noëlle

Education, Class Language and Ideology.
1. Educational equalization 2. Educational
sociology 3. Language and education
I. Title
370.19'3   LC213   78 40937

ISBN 0 7100 0118 5

Contents

Preface

The idea of this book arose during a seminar which Basil Bernstein asked me to give in June 1977 at the Institute of Education, University of London, of which he is the director. I am grateful to him for favouring the discussions between researchers and students on a problem which concerns everyone and not only researchers in the social sciences. I would also like to thank Diana Barker and Gella Skouras of the Institute of Education for the intellectual interest they have shown in this project of publication and the concrete help they have given in its realization.

I should like also to thank the following for their translations: Chapter 1, M. P. Eisele; Chapter 2, Diana Barker; Chapters 3 and 4, Catherine Cullen; Chapter 5, Philip Cullen.

Introduction

This book is a collection of five texts written between 1970 and 1971.[1] Its aim is to analyse, in relation to the problem of school selection, the efficacy of an ideology specific to class societies, essentialist ideology. An *effect* of concrete social relations, it is also an efficient *mediator* in what is called educability.

Ideology, the global system of interpretation through which a social formation explains its functioning to itself, is the *social discourse* on the world and on the human beings which social agents create at every moment through their set of practices (among which must be included the most apparently concrete practices, those which are 'obvious' to everyone — type of clothes and physical bearing — as well as symbolic practices — social categories as they are differentiated in dictionaries through the definition of 'woman' and 'man', 'black' and 'white', 'Jew' and 'Christian' etc.).

Thus the meaning accorded here to the word ideology is not as restrictive as the one usually adopted. Here ideology is understood not only as thoughts which have been crystallized in the form of theories, or as a system of explicit values, but also as a *system of practices*: motor and verbal behaviours as well as systematized mental productions. Ideology cannot be reduced either to reflexive knowledge or to representations, but is what is *enacted* beyond the models of intelligibility of social relationships accessible to man. Although ideology often takes the form of a conscious and rational speech on reality, it draws its dynamic strength from its unconscious dimension (as far as the unconscious is concerned, one should specify that the tangible reality necessarily articulated in language is what gives it its historically changing contents).

Essentialist ideology, which originates along with the establishment of those structures constituting class societies, is a denial of the *historical relations* of an economic, political, juridical and ideological order which preside over the establishment of labile power relationships. Essentialist ideology bases all social hierarchy on the transcendental principle of a natural biological order (which took over from a divine

1

principle at the end of the eighteenth century). A difference in essence among human beings supposedly predetermines the diversity of psychic and mental phenomena ('intelligence', 'language', etc.) and thus the place of individual in a social order considered as immutable.

A hidden referent of social discourse, a definition of 'Man', of 'Being' (based in fact on possession), is inherent to essentialist ideology. This referent has two dimensions: a concrete one, namely power such as is embodied in social beings defined by their practices; and a symbolic or imaginary dimension, power as it states its identity as a 'subject' and identity of others as 'objects'. This referent is one of the elements constituting the practices of the possessing-subjects and the depossessed-objects (whether these practices belong to the realm of doing or saying). Each social class cannot take on and shape its identity and give a meaning to its practices without referring to this dominant definition of being founded on having.

The different chapters of this book will show what essentialist ideology is and how it imposes a definition of their social identity on all social agents, whatever their position in the structure of power relationships. It bears an influence on an awareness of the determinisms at play in school selection, not only on common assumptions but also on attempts at scientific explanation.

Chapter 1 will specify the historical conditions of the origin of this ideology and will show that this ideology's explicit form has assumed a pseudo-scientific aspect through the first theory of scholastic inequalities, the theory of natural aptitudes. Through the speech of students, Chapter 2 will show the perpetuation of this ideology acting as a system of rationalization of school selection. But it will reveal the recent appearance of superficial changes in the traditional system of explanation; language differences and differences in aptitudes have become interchangeable elements.

This seems to contradict the appearance of a new scientific discourse, since the interest shown by researchers for language differences according to social class has coincided with a questioning of the scientific nature of the theory of aptitudes. In fact, the contradiction is only apparent. The thesis presented here is that the analysis of class languages has been undertaken without really breaking with the essentialist theories' metaphysical presuppositions. In order to show precisely where, in our view, this failure caused the attempt at theoretical reformulation to run aground, Chapter 3 proposes a new kind of approach to the relation between so-called popular linguistic forms and normative linguistic forms. It will show that one can grasp the meaning of the formal oppositions between class languages only if one does not ignore the power relations at work in linguistic practices themselves. By imposing the same social referent, essentialist ideology imposes the use of specific linguistic forms on each social class.

As they have ignored this fundamental point, scientific works — which have attempted to formulate, as opposed to discourse on aptitudes, an explicative theory of scholastic inequalities by basing them on linguistic differences — do not seem to have succeeded in bringing about the necessary epistemological rupture. B. Bernstein's work (Chapter 4) and that of P. Bourdieu and J. C. Passeron (Chapter 5) have been chosen as representative of two stages in a critical work which needs to be carried on.

Theoretical and terminological specifications

The fact that this book is centred on the analysis of ideological processes does not imply that the ideological phenomena have been abstracted and isolated from the other aspects of the social field, in particular that of economics. In fact, it represents a stage in research which began by revealing the socio-economic forces determining scholastic and occupational history (Chapter 2 summarizes its main results). In the course of this first phase of work, it became clear that studies on scholastic selection generally used criteria and terms which were directly generated by the dominant ideology, and which were far from neutral ('poor background', 'wealthy background', 'lower classes', 'upper classes', etc.). In fact, they suggest the idea of juxtaposed groups and thereby dissimulate what the social identity of these groups owes to dominance relationships.

What do *dominance relationships* mean? The term dominance[2] expresses a social relation between groups so that the one, the dominated group, is submitted to a system of real constraints by the other, the dominant group, in the economic, political, juridical and ideological spheres.

Dominance relationships, on which the functioning of the school system is based, imply the appropriation by a social group both of power in all its forms and of institutionalized knowledge. The knowledge passed on by the school system has become an instrument of economic domination[3] and a tool of ideological domination which ensures the permanence of the mode of production of class societies. In this respect, knowledge fulfils a function which is necessary on two accounts: on the one hand, the growth of productive forces involved in the mode of production relies above all on the possibilities of technical innovation allowed by the body of knowledge defined as science; on the other hand, the possession of knowledge which, from the nineteenth century, was perceived as the social sign of a biological superiority, has become an increasingly important means of legitimizing power, since right from the start its social effectiveness is interpreted as 'progress'.

The appropriation of knowledge and power in all its other forms lies at the basis of the existence of a dominated class and a dominant class.[4] Dominance relationships create sex classes according to the same processes of discrimination and hierarchization, as can be seen by the analysis of the facts of scholastic selection. The school system expresses and strengthens dominance relationships between social classes (in the classical sense of the word: position in the system of production based on a monetary economy) and between sex classes (social classes in which one would include – this is yet to be analysed – the production relations not based on a monetary economy). The fundamental question nowadays is precisely to elaborate a theory of the classes which takes into account the fact that dominance relationships between 'classes' and 'sexes' form a system, that sex classes exist, and that these classes are social. It will be seen that dominant ideology includes all the socially dominated in the same irrational definition.

Notes

1   The first text (Chapter 1) was published in English in *The Human Context*, vol. 3, 3, 1971, pp. 553–74. The second one (Chapter 2) was published in French in *Les Inégaux ou la sélection universitaire*, Paris, PUF, 1974, pp. 138–88. The text of Chapter 3 appeared in *L'Année sociologique*, vol. 25, 1975, pp. 237–64, under the title 'Langage et identité de classe, Les classes sociales "se" parlent'. Chapter 4 is a translation of the article 'Classes sociales et langage. Au-delà de la problématique privilège/handicap', *L'Homme et la société*, vols. 37–8, 1975, pp. 247–70. All these texts have been revised for the present publication. The last text (Chapter 5) was unpublished.

2   The word 'dominance' presents the advantage of emphasizing the *relationship*, whereas the term 'domination', due to its connotations, accentuates one of the sides of the relationship, the dominant group.

3   Economic dominance relationships can be defined as the social relations of production, distribution and consumption, based on the forms of appropriation and usage of the conditions of production and its result, the social product.

4   In our empirical studies, we have used the following criteria of class belonging: the occupation and level of education of the father, mother and four grandparents, and of the brothers and sisters; the number of children in the family, their geographic origins, and observations on the level of family resources. In the dominant class, we have included the owners of means of production and non-owners liable to invest a considerable fraction of the social

product which is allotted to them: industrialists, big businessmen, the liberal, scientific and artistic professions, all categories which appropriate valorized and useful knowledge. In the dominated class, we have included categories whose economic activity concerns either the dominant mode of production (industrial workmen) or modes of production which are on their way out (such as small farmers): agricultural workers, unskilled labourers, workers, domestic employees, small shop employees, or office employees. On a provisional basis, craftsmen, small shopkeepers and middle management have been grouped in the same category, but this grouping is not satisfactory. Traditionally called the middle class, these categories may be considered as functionally (and they are indeed indispensable as a cog in the wheel of power) but not structurally intermediary between the dominated and the dominant classes. They are the product of the fundamental relationship between the classes but do not modify it in any way.

1 Essentialist ideology. Its origins and its scientific form, the theory of natural aptitudes

According to a generally adopted system of interpretation, success or failure at school would be a manifestation of constitutional and hereditary intellectual aptitudes. This way of thinking is a part of Western culture; it arose at the end of the eighteenth century and took on a scientific language in the nineteenth century. When one tries to pinpoint the historical conditions in which this system, explanatory of social inequalities, appeared and survived, one sees that it goes along with the formation of class society structures in which the economic dimension is given primacy. The notion of aptitude is then disclosed as an element in an ideological system where social groups are perceived as static sets condemned to a natural destiny; they are not defined by the power relations that historically constituted them as antagonistic groups.

A comparison between the changes in meaning and use of that concept, and major events indicating overall changes in the economic, social, and political structures (as well as concomitant transformations of the educational system), evidences the growing importance of the word 'aptitude' from the eighteenth century onwards, when it was one with the concepts of 'merit' and 'individual responsibility' which are elements of the egalitarian ideology. While continuing to occupy a central position in the egalitarian ideology, the word changed its function radically in the wake of the French Revolution. Finally, it served as a justification of the unchanged social inequalities and concomitant educational inequalities, the latter being the result of the former and carrying them on at the same time. Since the new society and the educational institutions were held to be egalitarian, the root of these disparities could only be a 'natural' one. This justificatory ideology was progressively aided by scientific discoveries (anthropometry, first half of the nineteenth century; biology, second half of the nineteenth century; social sciences, end of the nineteenth century) which this ideology perpetually sought to re-interpret in the light of its own logic, and the approach of which it sometimes influenced.

In this sense, the present attempt at analysis of the concept of 'aptitude' is of an epistemological nature. In fact, the word 'aptitude' has already been studied, in view of conceptualization in a special branch of psychology, differential psychology, which having adopted this common-sense notion endeavours to define it scientifically. Scientific objectivity requires first and foremost a breaking away from certain forms of irrational thought, and second, a transmutation of ideological practice into theoretical practice.[1] However, the concept of aptitude is actually non-existent in most psychological theories which propose to set up a scientific corpus; only some research trends, founded on empirical practices (educational and vocational selection), call upon this concept; their approach is based on social demand whose interests are extra-scientific. Scientific investigation in this field is based on the explicit or implicit understanding that selection is necessary where there is social division of labour or social hierarchy, these being considered to be invariants, either absolutely or here and now. With its ideological preconceptions, this empirical practice is likely to come up with equally ideological findings instead of a corpus of scientific knowledge. The history of the term 'aptitude', its appropriation by one branch of psychology and its increasingly frequent use in educational reform projects as well as in current speech, will enable us to understand how this word has become the basic support and vehicle of an ideology that dates back to the nineteenth century and is still effective.

Prior to the nineteenth century, the word 'aptitude' designated a contingent reality

A legal term when it made its appearance in the fifteenth century,[2] 'aptitude' was synonymous with 'the quality of being fit for a position, or ability to come into a legacy'; hence this definition implied the idea of institution. Thereafter, it was taken up by philosophy, which introduced a new meaning, viz. a 'natural disposition to something'. Here the definition of aptitude implied Nature.[3] Now, Nature, which the society of the Ancien Régime held to be ordered by the will of God, was at that time the set of laws created by the Maker, and which governed both matter and mind according to a pre-established harmony. It is by divine decree that 'wood is more apt to be consumed by fire than stone' (Furetière, Trévoux), that somebody can have 'an aptitude for everything beautiful and good' (Richelet, Trévoux). Physical and mental deficiencies were the result of sin, of violation of a divine prohibition, but they were not irreversible, since they depended on divine grace, for 'miracles produce effects over and above the forces of Nature, and are not a result of natural laws' (Furetière). However, the gift of God, aptitude, conferred no superiority of rank.[4] Effectual power was linked to birth: man is born 'powerful' or 'miserable' and remains so all his life, by the Will of God; the 'quality' or 'condition' did not depend at all on mental or physical aptitudes. Up to the end of the eighteenth century, the use of the word 'aptitude' was rare in everyday language; it was a pendantic world, according to most of the seventeenth-century dictionaries, a 'barbarism' to Father Bouhours, arbiter of the Court's conventional language; in the eighteenth century, it was ranked by Abbé Prévost among the 'French words whose meaning is not familiar to everybody'; at the same period, Trévoux's dictionary mentions that it 'has a fragrance of Latin'.

The term came into use in the course of the second half of the eighteenth century, at a time when the references to 'Nature' no longer implied the former theocentric conception. Though the aristocracy continued to exercise its power by virtue of divine right, those whom it looked down upon for being employed were getting an increasingly powerful grip on Nature: they invented the steam engine, discovered electricity, exploited the mines of Anzin, of Le Creusot, mechanized the production of textiles and metals, instigated the establishment of the first Grandes Ecoles: Ponts-et-Chaussées and Mines. The relation between man and the world was changed by this progressive control over Nature: man no longer expected God to intervene in the course of events by miracles. The material and human world was governed by its own laws to be discovered by Science. Naturalists endeavoured to re-integrate man into the continuum of the physical universe and the living species; they were, therefore, led to classify him by distinctive physical characteristics, and to investigate these differences; some like Lamarck altogether discarded the fixist view in which the order of things had been set once and for all by the Will of God. Similarly, the attention paid to psychical features, in other words to abilities, tended to become a search for laws. Gall probed into the intelligence of various species by ascending the scale of animals up to man, and tried to determine relevant areas in the brain corresponding to each ability.[5] Since, in the eighteenth century, man had become the central point of reference, his mental and physical particularities were hence investigated in a relativist perspective. Differences between human groups or individuals were found to be contingent and relative to the physical or social environment. This scientific activity, this control over the world, and the new form which this self-investigation of man took on during that period, was particular to a social class which was becoming increasingly self-conscious. By eliminating God, it wanted to master its destiny. The bourgeoisie wielded economic, though not political, power.[6] That is why it challenged the prevalent social order, in which position was determined by birth. It related the inequalities of destiny to social institutions and claimed political power on the strength of individual merit.

The definitions of the word 'aptitude' at that period reflect this change in social relations. On the one hand, the meaning of the word was specified in reference to actual human activities: 'One is said to have, or not to have, a great aptitude for mathematics, poetry, painting, etc.' (Abbé Féraud); on the other hand, although aptitude was still defined as a 'natural disposition', this definition no longer reflected the initial meaning: Abbé Féraud illustrated it with the saying: 'Nurture transcends Nature' ('*Nourriture passe nature*'); 'education has greater power over us than even Nature; habits create a second nature; they have as much (and even sometimes more) power over us than our natural inclinations.' Thus an individual owed his aptitude to perform certain tasks to the random fact of being born in a given environment. This explains the passionate interest in the new pedagogical tendencies of the day; Itard endeavoured to apply concretely Rousseau's and Condorcet's ideas, and to show that past experience does not determine the psychical frame of an individual once and for all; he applied himself to proving that the idiocy of the Wild Boy of Aveyron was reversible and not definitive.

At the outbreak of the Revolution, the facts seemed to confirm the conviction that social organization was in the hands of man and not God or Nature, for it had been possible to overthrow the social order which the nobles had set up to their benefit. The Law was empowered to found a new social order, by offering to everybody without discrimination the theoretical possibility of physical, intellectual, and moral development to the greatest benefit of a society which, after getting rid of its inequalities, would be able to achieve enormous progress. When, in response to a precise wish formulated for the first time in 1762, the Constituante proclaimed the principle of a 'public education common to all citizens, and free with respect to those parts of education which are indispensable for all men', it was founding its greatest hopes of equalization of opportunities on educational institutions. After Condorcet's and Talleyrand's reform projects, the *écoles primaires d'état* (state primary schools) were set up by the decree of 21 October 1793. A little later, Lakanal established the *écoles centrales* (technical universities) and the *écoles normales*; the *Grandes Ecoles* were being reorganized, and others founded, such as the *École Polytechnique*. All these educational institutions were called upon to advance the sciences and to enable each individual to fulfil to the best of his capacities the social functions called for by progress.

One of these essential functions was precisely that of educating the people. Since the most urgent task was to achieve national unity by rallying people round a common language, there was a great need for finding 'able' teachers, i.e. people who knew the local idiom or dialect and were able to teach French and the new metric system. So one spoke of selection for entrance into the *écoles normales* in terms of pedagogical aptitudes. There was a general demand for teachers with 'talent', 'dispositions', 'abilities' and 'aptitudes', as transpires from the 'Lettres à Grégoire',[7] and the projects of popular societies.[8] Aptitude, formerly a gift of God, was now considered to be an eminently changeable result of environment and education; moreover, it was invested with a new value by which certain social functions could be claimed, and yet everybody was proclaimed to have equal rights, whatever his functions. One no longer talked of the 'lower people', or of the 'lower classes', but already of the 'People', and of the 'working class'.[9] The word 'worker' was losing its pejorative connotation. Whereas in the seventeenth century a 'worker' was 'somebody of abject condition' (P. Bouhours), in the eighteenth century the word was considered 'vulgar' (*bas dans le propre*) (Abbé Féraud); but after the Revolution in 1801 de Wailly[10] offered a neutral definition of the word, viz. somebody 'who works with his hands': a sign of certain changes in the human relations. The bourgeoisie, which had called on the people whom it wanted to instruct in order to strip the nobles of their privileges, strongly believed that, while correcting the intolerable inequalities to its advantage, it was rebuilding an egalitarian society. But in fact, concerned with its own interest, it set up to its profit another social hierarchy which engendered new inequalities: political inequalities, since the so-called universal suffrage excluded women and servants; economic inequalities, since it established the regime of private property; educational inequalities, since according to Condorcet 'secondary schools are established for children whose parents can devote a larger number of years to their education.'[11] Now, although inequalities prevailed, the principle of equality nevertheless gained universal recognition. Instead of birth and divine right, notions of equality, merit, aptitude, competence and individual responsibility rallied round a comprehensive ideology, to which the 'People' adhered as well.

The first half of the nineteenth century: 'aptitude' becomes an essential hereditary feature: birth of a new ideology justifying social inequalities

After many difficulties which the country, ravaged by civil strife and foreign wars, had to cope with, the bourgeoisie succeeded in taking political power; the year 1830 opened up the era of the 'bourgeois conquerors'.[12] Thanks to the war and the Napoleonic blockade, the French economy was able, on the one hand, to absorb the mass of unemployed manpower, and, on the other, to reinforce its position opposite that of the English by taking advantage of a Continental market, as it was opened up by the Napoleonic conquest. During the Restoration and under the July Monarchy, a new boost was given to the economy: the metal industry grew in the Massif Central, in the East and in the North, textile concerns emerged, roads and railways were built, and allegorical figures of Industry and Commerce were to decorate palaces and newspaper headings. The manpower which had become available by the end of the wars was immediately taken up by the many sectors of a rapidly expanding economy. A new social hierarchy emerged. As a class the aristocracy vanished; the Tiers-Etat broke up into two classes: the ruling bourgeoisie and the proletariat, to which the former, to all intents and purposes, refused voting rights on account of property-linked suffrage (*suffrage censitaire*), i.e. suffrage linked to wealth. Although the proletariat, frustrated in its revolutionary hopes, continued to call for real equality, and, as is witnessed by Proudhon's ideas, started to hammer out its own ideology, the bourgeoisie, which had benefited from the overthrow of the former order, envisaged equality only with reference to members of its own class. It believed that the natural course of events would gradually settle any social problems which the State did not want to tackle. Whereas it claimed State assistance to its advantage (to finance the construction of railways to be run by private enterprise), it categorically refused such assistance to workers in the name of the imperatives of economic progress, and in the name of individual liberty.

The claims of clubs and popular societies for a generalized primary education were gradually silenced. Primary education, neglected by Napoleon, was reorganized and provided with a budget for the first time in 1833; but it was denominational, neither free, nor compulsory, and for boys only.[13] The interest of reformers focused on secondary education reserved for children of rich families. The issue which over the whole nineteenth century animated debates and oriented successive reforms was whether to teach humanities or science. A strong demand from private industry had to be coped with, hence the foundation, in 1829, of the *Ecole Centrale des Arts et Manufactures*, and the expansion around 1832 of the first vocational training institutions (*écoles d'arts et métiers*). In the face of traditionalists, the innovators, mindful of the country's economic development, started to use the justificatory principle of the diversity of aptitudes. In 1852, Fortoul referred to this in his reform project which aimed at setting up two secondary options, one literary, the other scientific. However, all this concerned only the ideological debate which divided the same social class – the bourgeoisie – about what type of person to train in order to form an 'élite' for a society which was undergoing a radical transformation. The debate concerned only children of this class.[14]

Confronted with the tangible inequalities it had maintained after taking the political power and strengthening its hold on economic power, the bourgeoisie was to develop an ideology by which it could justify these disparities and silence an opposition which threatened its newly acquired privileges. This confrontation was all the more vital for the bourgeoisie as it could not deny the principle of equality in the name of which it had claimed power from the noblesse. The bourgeoisie therefore constantly proclaimed that everybody was free and equal by law and that the destiny of man no longer depended on an established social order but on individual capacities. Thus, the bourgeoisie consolidated itself as a class by denying to those whom it subjected to its political and economic power the essential qualities of intelligence, merit, and responsibility, of which it availed itself and which justified its power. Anthropometrical research was to confirm this ideology through scientific findings. Physical anthropology and craniometry aroused increasing interest: Maximilien Parchappe developed a craniometrical method which spread rapidly through the world: 'there is no doubt', he wrote in 1848,[15] 'that the organic difference which most surely expresses the innate difference in the intellectual scope of individuals of the human species is that of the volume of the brain, the organ of thinking.' This is an hereditary feature, and 'this hereditary resemblance between children and parents concerns not only physical and organic characteristics of height, form, and colour, it also extends to behaviour, gait, the sound of voice, intellectual aptitudes, and moral character.' It is this heredity complex which confers the particular aptitudes that determine social rank, for it was well understood that in modern States, whose constitutions are based on the principles of individual freedom and civil equality, 'the distribution of social functions is spontaneous'. In the United States at the same period Nott and Gliddon tried to show, on the basis of their anthropometrical findings, that Negroes and Europeans were of different origin, that the former were inferior to the latter, and destined to serve them.

Thus, explanatory schemata were developed to account for social differences and inequalities in the very name of an egalitarian ideology. Prior to Darwin and to the investigation into hereditary mechanisms, a justificatory system of social inequalities on the grounds of natural aptitudes and their hereditary character was already well established. This fundamental postulate which attributed the basis of psychological and cultural differences to the observed physical and biological differences was to gain considerable influence.[16] In 1830, 'intelligent' was a very fashionable word indeed. Intelligence, according to Laveaux's dictionary, is 'a certain straightforwardness of the soul which perceives what is true and just, and keeps to it'. He said in a different passage, 'a worker [. . .] is somebody who has a mechanical occupation which does not require any intelligence.'[17] Intelligence, and aptitude for the study of science or the arts, became attributes of children of the bourgeoisie, which restricted the size of its families in order to provide its offspring with a maximum of education and to pass on to them its entire economic patrimony. The connotations of the term aptitude therefore progressively came to designate unchangeable, permanent, hereditary data which determined the destiny of an individual; thus, 'aptitude' lost the random connotation it had both in the eighteenth century with the idea of human freedom, and before the eighteenth century with the idea of divine freedom.

The second half of the nineteenth century: 'Aptitude' refers to a strictly biological causal process. The word 'becomes a part of everyday language'

The suppression of the revolt of the proletariat in 1848 ushered in a new era which was to witness the triumph of industry and the expansion of trade. As to industry, steel production, which the new technical inventions had rendered possible, was going to act as the same driving force as cotton had done in the previous century. Roads, canals, railways, telegraphic networks covered Europe; colonization opened up new promising markets; banking circuits were established, corporations set up, financial and industrial concentrations multiplied. The division of labour brought about multiple and hierarchized tasks and a real administration of the economy emerged with a need for technically trained people on all levels.

In order to cope with the needs of a country in full economic expansion, and with a social demand emanating from the lower middle class situated between the bourgeoisie and the proletariat, in 1865 Victor Duruy set up a secondary, so-called 'special' teaching sector with a view to training specialists for the industrial, commercial and rural sectors. Schools of commerce and agriculture sprang up after 1870. Nevertheless, the need to teach the people was increasingly felt: in 1867 (i.e. 34 years after the institution of primary education for boys), the State imposed on local governments (the Communes) the obligation to set up primary schools for girls; in 1881, primary education became free, non-denominational and compulsory. The bourgeoisie, however, for distinction's sake, called upon parallel and fee-paying primary schooling: the elementary grades of the lycée. Similarly, heated ideological debates on Latin and the humanities, which were to lead the way to modern education and establish the principle of a single stream of secondary education with classical and modern options, masked the profound difference deliberately established between secondary education reserved for bourgeois children, and primary education left to the 'people'. According to Jules Ferry, by means of this primary education 'boys were to be prepared for future employment as workers and soldiers, and girls for housekeeping and women's handicrafts.' There were, it is true, the higher primary schools (*écoles primaires supérieures*), enabling some to go beyond the elementary level, but, as F. Buisson and Jules Ferry made it clear, the type of teaching dispensed in these institutions must resist the seductions of a general-type education. The educational system itself therefore actively maintained the superiorities and privileges of the dominant class.

The system of beliefs, in the name of which this class sought to justify social inequalities, was being strengthened by developments in biology. In this respect the work of Darwin had a considerable effect, for the idea of vital competition producing a natural selection and the survival of the fittest was indeed closely related to the ideology of a 'spontaneous distribution of social functions' (Parchappe). Social disparities were no longer relative to a man-made social order, but belonged to a new transcendental order of an irreducible and determinant biological nature. Men were categorized by the same criteria of differentiation as those applied to animal-breeding and agriculture, which supplied Darwin with the principles for his theory. Gobineau systematized this diffuse ideology in 1852 by his *Essai sur l'inégalité des races humaines*. This is the first explicitly racist theory which demonstrates scientifically that the hierarchy of societies and social classes is based on biological differentiation. The domination of some by others was therefore natural, inevitable, and legitimate. Some societies have 'an aptitude for indefinite intellectual development'; those who lack this aptitude are free to try and imitate the others, but 'imitation is no proof of the existence of a serious break with hereditary tendencies.' The same is true of social classes: 'in a nation of composite essence, civilization does not exist at all social levels. While the ancient ethnic causes continue to act at the bottom of the social scale, they admit or allow penetration by the ruling national genius only slightly and sporadically.' Education of 'rurals and workers', which is dangerous for the social order and the future of civilization, is useless and inefficient: 'I would therefore approve with greater ease of mind so many generous efforts which are wasted on the education of our rural populations, if I were not convinced that the latter are not fit for the knowledge they are given.'

Some time later, Tylor and Morgan were to set up their theory of social and cultural evolutionism: their own society, which was considered the most perfect and most accomplished society, served as the central reference point for the classification and ordering of the different cultural systems.

The basic metaphysical presupposition of evolutionist theories, which led Gobineau to reduce social inequalities to determinant psycho-biological differences (whether he was comparing different societies or different classes), equally influenced the theories of F. Galton, the father of differential psychology. A relative of Darwin, on whom his ideas were to have a great influence, Galton undertook to show by means of a new scientific method that mental differences belong to the same order as difference in height, and are equally hereditary. Quételet, who first applied Gauss's findings regarding the laws of probability to the social sciences, established that the height of individuals follows a normal curve; Galton inferred on the basis of this postulate that mental faculties were to follow the same sort of curve. The method of correlation by which he measured the degree of relationship between mental and physical aptitudes on the one hand, and parents' and children's aptitudes on the other, enabled him to 'verify' the natural and hereditary character of aptitudes. 'I propose to show in this book that a man's natural abilities are derived by inheritance, under exactly the same limitations as are the form and physical features of the whole organic world', he wrote in the introduction to his famous book, *Hereditary Genius.*[18] For him, as for Gobineau, the human species was degenerating and therefore needed improvement through appropriate selection in order to obtain 'a highly-gifted race of men by judicious marriages during several consecutive generations'. Galton's constitutionalist postulate (he was the father of both eugenics and differential psychology) was going to weigh heavily on this branch of psychology.[19] Gall's psycho-biological parallelism became a biological determinism of psychological and social life. Thus in social science research one can trace the patterns of thought by which the bourgeoisie apprehended social reality.[20]

However, the idea of a distribution of aptitudes that was unequal by nature, and whereby individuals were irrevocably given a place on the social scale, was gradually seriously questioned. Great social conflicts were breaking out. The working class got organized, and, in 1864, obtained the right to strike. In 1867, a serious economic slump triggered off a powerful wave of strikes. Marx published his *Capital* in the same year. The International, which took up some of his ideas that ran radically counter to those of his time, assumed a leading role in the workers' movement. In 1871, the social order was seriously shaken and momentarily overthrown by the Commune. Social disparities did not appear so naturally determined to everybody. In fact, as Durkheim put it, 'the link is broken in a whole sphere of society between individual aptitudes and the kind of activity actually assigned to and exercised by individuals; it is only by pure, more or less violent and direct constraints that they are tied down to their functions.'[21] Hence the idea spread among those who wanted to maintain the social order that social conflicts could be resolved by psychology: this science should be able to detect 'true' latent aptitudes, on the basis of which each individual would be assigned his right place in society.

15

Such were the preoccupations of the first psychologists who sought to measure intelligence. Binet, who wanted to improve employer-employee relations, dreamt of an ideal city 'in which the social climate would be better than in ours, in which everyone would work according to his recognized aptitude with the effect that no morsel of psychological force would be lost to society.'[22] The metrical intelligence scale which he developed put liberals, set on social justice, in a position to found their hopes on this new science – the psychology of tests. In 1903, school teachers started a revolutionary trade unionist movement, *L'Ecole émancipée*. Similarly, young teachers joined forces at the end of the First World War to found the Movement of the *Compagnons de l'Université Nouvelle*, and to claim the suppression of distinctions of social origin which barred the access to secondary and higher educational institutions. It was the first educational reform project that explicitly proposed educational selection on the basis of aptitudes. This proposition certainly stemmed from a generous movement on the part of those who were concerned with social progress and who were shocked at the institutionalized segregation of children by social origin. The factual situation made it quite plain what sort of ideology caused segregation, since the enrolment in higher primary schools and complementary classes already exceeded enrolment rates in the lycées, and since the gaps caused by the war in the different sectors of activity and on the different hierarchical levels called for an enlargement of recruitment procedures. However, the distribution of aptitudes which reformers wanted to use for selecting entrants into a secondary-level *école unique* was not a result of chance. In fact, Binet found that 'the intellectual level of children varies according to the affluence of the population.'[23] Equal opportunity of access to the *école unique* was therefore seriously questionable.

It should be noted, in fact, that towards the end of the nineteenth century, the words 'aptitude' and 'selection', on the basis of which these reformers wanted to found a juster society, had acquired a new meaning, which those who used them could not be fully aware of. The expression 'selection', which necessarily implied valuation criteria, was taken from the language of agriculture and animal-breeding. Research on the processes of fertilization had made it possible to exploit Mendel's discoveries, which had not attracted attention in 1865, the main target being the improvement of livestock and animal selection to achieve a maximum yield. The scientific discoveries in the field of biology sustained and confirmed already well-established patterns of thought according to which the relation between biological and psychological facts was of a causal order, the first explaining the second. Genetics, which was making considerable advances, served as a theoretical basis for the idea of hereditary transmission of mental aptitudes. In current language, the word 'aptitude', 'today of common usage', as Littré noted at the end of the nineteenth century,[24] inherited a biologistic meaning of which dictionary definitions give evidence. In the Littré, the diction- ary of cultured people (as in the Larousse designed for autodidacts), the contiguity of psychological and 'agronomical' definitions is indica- tive of the unconscious mixture of two orders, viz. aptitude as 'a natural propensity for mathematics', next to aptitude, 'a natural dis- position to yield a lot of milk, etc.'. Aptitude, heredity, selection form part of the same semantic field at a time when educational needs were growing.

The age of tests: aptitude as a measurable reality. The science of aptitudes as the warrant of a legitimate social order

Binet's research on intelligence caused a wave of interest which was not unrelated to its possible practical implications. His first clinical investiga- tions on the genesis of the higher intellectual processes led him to dis- cover a variability of forms of judgment and reasoning which only the social environment of the young children whom he tested could account for. The Ministry of Public Instruction of the day, which was greatly interested in these findings, asked Binet to develop an instrument liable to detect which children were unable to follow a normal primary course.[25] So Binet abandoned his scientific investigations, which would have enabled him to study the causes of the differences he had noted, and particularly to circumscribe the role of 'social influence, like that of neediness or sheer poverty of large families'.[26] He progressively turned to a purely empirical scientific practice which he later came to regret. His research on the processes of judgment and reasoning, in which he relativized the notion of intelligence, was superseded by the con- struction of a metrical intelligence scale, which aimed at the establish- ment of norms on the basis of an individual's use in society. Age was the major criterion in terms of which performance and its deviation from normality were gauged. Now, this age valuation was not alien to the field in which Binet was working, viz. that of the educational system, where, as soon as the principle of compulsory schooling had been accepted, the performance requirements of each grade were decided after fixing the first year and terminal year age. Educational and social standards, by which 'precocity' was positively and retarded- ness negatively rated, became and remained the central reference upon which research on mental age, intelligence quotient, and developmental psychology was based.

As stated earlier, some years after Binet's research on intelligence measurement, reform projects of secondary education following the

First World War referred to selection on the strength of aptitude. Selection was mentioned for the first time together with the claim for an enlargement of social recruitment. However, neither economic stringencies, nor the situation of the educational system, imposed such a necessity as yet; the number of lycée enrolments, for which tuition fees were payable, remained unchanged for years and intakes were limited to bourgeois children. There was no question of gauging their aptitudes, or barring their entrance to lycées. However, Binet's findings were immediately applied in countries such as the USA, where the general ideology of progress, efficiency, and productivity immediately found application in selective practices. A major target was to get a predictive tool; test standard conformity was considered a guarantee of healthy adaptation to the educational system and unquestionable social success. The more the tests gave correct predictions the more the reality of what had been measured, namely aptitudes, was evidenced. Only natural aptitude, considered as diverse and fundamentally unequal, could explain the differentiation and hierarchization of individuals and social groups. The reference to aptitude can justify differences in educational opportunities and, consequently, social disparities, since the school is supposed to offer each individual the same opportunities to give evidence of his 'true' verbal, numerical, mnemonic, and other abilities.

These psychologists generally failed to recognize the relativity of standards which governed their own social system (and were victims of the same universalist illusion as were the seventeenth- and eighteenth-century philosophers); they were generally very uncritical regarding the system of values which influenced their dividing up of reality, and which they used to perform their job of differentiating individuals: they attempted to trace the essence of Man's aptitudes at large, without being aware of the restrictive manner in which they defined him. At about the same time, ethnologists, who were undertaking the same sort of investigation, became aware of the impact of social institutions on the genesis of mental and psychological structures. Doubtless, psychologists are less detached than ethnologists with respect to the object of their studies; indeed, the latter investigate small, enclosed, distant societies, with which their own society has no organic links; this is not the case of 'aptitudes researchers', who are interested in their own cultural system and are themselves deeply involved in the social pattern in which the categories and individuals they perceive as different are organically entwined. The categories of sex and the aptitudes attributed to men and women, the categories of class and the degree of general intelligence attributed to 'low' and 'high' classes, the categories of 'race', and abilities assigned thereto operate like an unconscious frame of reference in the researchers's attempt at self-definition. Their own position in the social system to which they belong, and their 'race', class, and sex characteristics, bear on their apprehension of others, and govern their scientific work. Cultural ethnocentrism, which is evident in the belief in the existence of human aptitudes at large, is paralleled by an ethnocentricity deriving from the dominant position psychologists hold in their own society. The others, i.e. those who do not possess the qualities attributed to those holding a dominant position, are defined by a lack; they are characterized by the absence of complex, first-rate aptitudes.

Hence the hierarchy of aptitudes follows the pattern of the social hierarchy: general intelligence (factor G) is the attribute of the ruling class; specific and limited abilities characterize manual workers. Research on intellectual performance has consequently given rise to ever more refined analyses resulting in a huge repertoire of aptitudes set out in a complex structure; in a second phase, the attempt was made to understand the unequal distribution of these aptitudes by means of huge representative samplings of the population. On the other hand, research on job requirements for the execution of so-called manual tasks generally followed an atomistic approach. Here, scientific interest seemed no longer to care about an overall picture of all the various aptitudes involved, or the complexity of their structure. *A priori*, these tasks, which were supposed to call only for an inferior, so-called 'practical', 'mechanical' form of intelligence, required only specific aptitudes, such as 'manual dexterity', etc.[27]

Finally, if aptitudes and their structure are meant to explain the behaviour of individuals, the degree of intelligibility conferred by the use of the concept of aptitude is not the same for all the social classes to which it is applied; some possess complex aptitudes, set out in a hierarchical order, others are negatively defined, by the lack of any valued aptitude.[28] Thus, the 'intelligent' class only discovers the 'natural' specific aptitudes of the class 'incapable of intellectual tasks' when these aptitudes have a practical bearing, in relation to the needs of the labour market. The ideal would be to match specific aptitudes with job requirements as they result from the division of labour.[29] Although some researchers continue to enquire into the nature of their scientific object, as will be seen, most of those working in the field seem little concerned with theory or with an analysis of what they are actually measuring with their tools.[30] The scientific question becomes a question relative to educational and vocational policies; the 'proven' efficiency of tests in this field justifies an empirical practice which is not disturbed by the problem of the ideology on which it rests. Opening up new possibilities, the science of tests attains two targets which are difficult to reconcile: to offer equal chances to all on the one hand, and to maintain social and vocational status inequalities on the other. Once the small fringe of 'over intelligent' people at the bottom of the social

scale has been sifted out in order to maintain social justice, every man
will be in his right place in society. The study of aptitudes thus becomes
the scientific warrant of a social organization which it justifies.

Scientific definitions of the concept of aptitude. A criticism of the relevance of its use in the social sciences. Permanence of a nineteenth-century pattern of thought

After borrowing from common language this concept loaded with metaphysical implications that had accumulated over the years, differential
psychology endeavoured to purify its meaning while using it as a conceptual tool for its theoretical practice. Some definitions are authorita-
tive, to judge by quotations and source references in specialized, as well
as in current, dictionaries, and by the legitimation which the educational
system confers upon them through its teachers, viz. its agents for the
distribution of established knowledge. Thus, *inter alia*, the *Vocabulaire
technique et critique de la philosophie* by A. Lalande, the *Dictionnaire
alphabétique et analogique de la langue française* by P. Robert, the
bibliographical lists recommended to psychology students all refer to a
book by Claparède which indeed had an international readership and
exerted great influence.[31]

The basis on which Claparède sought to give a scientific definition
of the concept of aptitude is that of social practice, viz. educational and
vocational selection. The failure of his attempt was not altogether unrelated to this normative approach. Although he held that 'all our
psychological activities [. . .] are the result of both heredity and
environment', his naturalistic presuppositions led him rapidly to drop
'environment' altogether. He argued somewhat naïvely from commonsense experience and 'proof' that 'everything being equal in other
respects [. . .] two individuals show different aptitudes. There is hence
something innate, natural about it [. . .].' Environmental factors which
were later to be called 'exogenous or extrinsic' represented the contingent element, the epi-phenomenon, which had to be reduced in order to
study the 'natural' phenomena in their original purity; they had to be
'eliminated', they 'biassed' the determination of aptitudes for diagnosis.
This amounted to Claparède's endorsing the common-usage definition
offered by Littré ('we use the word aptitude – as it should be used –
only for a natural disposition'). Nevertheless the obviousness of this
definition should have been a warning to the scientist as to the degree
of his blindness. For, if ambiguity tainted both his definition of aptitude
and his use, it was because Claparède, along with most psychologists of
his day, used this concept as a being rather than a function or a tool.

Later on, a terminological controversy opposed Christiaens, for whom aptitude was a developmental result of the exercise of a 'native disposition', to Piéron, who blamed him for 'calling abilities aptitudes' and wanted to use the latter exclusively for the 'inborn substratum', which is pre-existent to ability.[32] However, the idea that individual differences have biological causes was patently shared by both authors. Naturally, theories which transformed the field of psychological knowledge, such as psychoanalytical theory, Gestalt-theory, behaviourism, culturalism, phenomenology (theories where the concept of aptitude has no place), could not but affect knowledge relating to the causes of individual differences. Reference to a bipolar scheme, taking into due account the respective influence of 'heredity' and 'environment', has now replaced the former causal theory, which reduces psychological to biological facts.

However, one of these poles is still considered as more important. The theory of individual differences, on which the empirical practice of test methods relies, persists in borrowing its explanatory patterns from biology. Thus, H. Piéron considers that intelligence 'depends primarily on hereditary aptitude'.[33] For C. Burt, 'intelligence depends directly on the neuronic structure, hence there are strong assumptions in favour of the view that it is determined by genetical influences, like almost all physiological phenomena.'[34] Such is the postulate which governs the choice, the analysis, and the interpretation of data. The phrase 'everything being equal in other respects . . .', and the oversimplification of what is understood by 'environmental factors' in general, are significant of this postulate. 'Environmental', that eternal disrupter, without which the apprehension of actual natural aptitudes would be very simple, was considered as a physical reality, producing purely mechanical effects. These effects, arbitrarily called 'contingent', are of the same kind as those to which test animals in laboratories are exposed, whenever conditions governing the transmission of a genotype or the appearance of various phenotypes are to be established. It seems to be the reference to these experimental projects that determines *a priori* reasoning applied to the case of twins: the 'same' family and social environment must produce identical effects. Because of an uncritical acceptance of the belief that intelligence is transmitted via genes, there is no conception of the fact that there are specific dynamics at work in each individual from his birth all along the way, and consequently no understanding of the Freudian contribution. Research focusing on the discovery of primary causes entailing mental, psychological, and social facts in a linear and irreversible order has been governed by ethical considerations, which influenced its applications. Following Galton and the nineteenth-century philosophers, the issues are now governed by political considerations: 'if, ultimately, it so happened,' wrote C. Burt, 'that the views of the pioneers were approximately correct [. . .] the impact of genetic variations on our present national and social difficulties would be only too obvious.'

However, reflection on the basic principles, determining standardizing procedures for selection and vocational guidance tests, led some researchers to the conclusion that the concept of aptitude itself does not make much sense. In 1945, P. Naville forcefully criticized the theory of aptitudes by refuting its metaphysical postulates.[35] He pointed out that 'the opposition between natural and acquired dispositions is purely verbal; it is a mere opposition of words, denoting a sort of incapacity, which is proper to so many other psychological fields, for stating the simple dialectical relations which make up the texture of our real activity [. . .] In fact, it would be more appropriate to talk of adaptitude rather than of aptitude.' His criticism relies on facts, which a precise sociological analysis enabled him to bring out and which show that 'the practice of vocational guidance narrowly follows economic needs which derive from requirements of the ruling classes.' Later on, some differential psychologists, in their turn, questioned the concept of aptitude. In 1954, M. Reuchlin[36] vigorously criticized this scientific pseudo-concept in an article whose significant title, 'The Use of Aptitudes', at once called out for questions such as: of whom? by whom? what for? As he points out, some psychologists are blinded by the normal distribution of measurements they obtain and forget that these distributions actually are conditioned by test construction and standardizing procedures; they then 'assimilate test results to aptitudes which are considered stable constitutional characteristics.' While criticizing the metaphysical principles underlying the search for these basic characteristics, the author concludes by recalling the need for going beyond common language concepts, such as that of aptitude.

Nowadays, research on 'cognitive styles' is the new form taken by research on aptitudes. Some researchers, whether they discard the concept of aptitude altogether, or whether they give it the meaning of physical or psychical characteristics by which a given task can be realized without any fixed postulate, apply themselves to describing differences between individuals or groups; they temporarily avoid the causal question. They strive to find out whether certain groups get better test scores than others, or show a better learning performance, without caring about the reasons for such a difference in performance. Nevertheless, the very construction of what is to be studied, and the choice of tests, necessarily supposes the reference to established standards and values prevailing in a given social system.[37] It should be noted in passing that this object of study within a given social system is constructed in such a way as to cope with certain social needs, defined *a priori*, and in respect of which researchers are concerned with explicit, practical targets.

On the other hand, most differential psychologists engaged in research, concerned as they are with the identification of 'dimensions' and their organization in the legitimate hope of someday discovering the general pattern of behaviour, exclude from their scientific practice any analysis of the social conditions under which the differential behaviour of individuals emerges.[38] The genesis of behaviour proper to the different social categories considered is not alien to the fact that these categories are already specified as different within the society as a whole. Now, present investigation is limited in the following way: the components of intelligence and their patterns are studied but no account is taken of the social definition of categories whose test-achievement is expected to be different, nor of how these categories are socially structured. While criticizing the atomistic and realistic approach of 'faculty' psychology, a similar approach is adopted when age, sex, 'race', social 'environment' are accepted as sheer commonsense evidence.[39] Yet precisely, for society at large, children and adults, men and women, black and white, bourgeois and proletarians are different by 'nature', as has been well analysed by C. Guillaumin.[40] The irreversibility, the fixedness, the immutability that were to be avoided are thus unconsciously reintroduced into the thinking process: the social categories on which the analysis of differential characteristics is founded, are essentialized instead of simply being relatively defined in terms of their actual and symbolic interrelations.

The underlying, and often unconscious, postulate is that the physical characteristics of a category designated by a lack (of white skin, a phallus, motional or verbal facility, etc.) necessarily entail mental and psychological characteristics which lack those dimensions which are the sign of superiority and of belonging to the ruling 'élite'. The research approach chosen evidences this postulate: first the attempt is made to work out tests outside any social context,[41] then these tests are applied to clearly distinct social groups; as a result, it is noted that these groups are indeed psychologically different, that their intelligence indeed varies in degree and nature. These differences are naturally no longer considered, at least explicitly, to be the reason for the social differences. On the contrary, emphasis is laid on the weight of economic and cultural constraints that condition the factual and symbolic behaviour of social groups and their members, and it is pointed out in particular that society does not use all available intellectual resources, since a number of poor-class children of 'superior' intelligence have actually no chance to pursue their studies. But, whatever the ethical views of authors, the mere fact that they restrict themselves to noting unequal statistical distribution of intellectual aptitudes by 'race', sex, and social class, and exclude the study of the genesis of behaviour specific to certain social categories which lack socially prized qualities, results in strengthening the ideology by which the dominant group owes its power simply to its natural superiority, since it is implied that these categories are different by 'nature'.

If there is no way out of this problem, it is because differential psychology defines its object only in terms of social applications. The first concern is either to bring about the best possible adaptation of individuals or groups to the educational and occupational system, or to prove the necessity for pedagogical reforms whereby the gifted children of 'poor' classes should also be selected. Social practice as marked by the targets of technocratic planning shows the way for scientific practice. The latter, which is a result of the rejection of constitutionalist postulates, purports to be essentially descriptive, but the descriptive method can be fruitful only if the findings serve to prop up a theory which is considered valid for a given state of knowledge. If the theoretical issue at stake is that of the respective influence of 'heredity' and 'environment' on the genesis of mental and psychical phenomena, the mere noting of individual differences on the basis of synchronic studies (even if they are repeated regularly) cannot be a substitute for the analysis of the processes involved; this analysis may be complex, it is nevertheless necessary with regard to the issue. This mistake is due to the approach adopted and the postulate on which it is implicitly founded, namely that of the existence of an essential reality.

In conclusion, emphasis is laid on the permanence of the nineteenth-century pattern of thought, which has striven to account for social inequalities by natural inequalities. The educational system is one of the privileged places where it is possible to grasp how this class ideology has progressively been translated into operative practice, and how great has been its impact on the overall system of thought. Demographic, economic, technical, and political upheavals, which shook the whole social system in the wake of the Second World War, ushering in a new age of economic planning, also affected the whole educational system by upsetting its balance. When, consequently, the need for educational reforms was urgently felt, the ideology of aptitudes exerted a particularly strong influence on decision-making. At a time when social demand started pressing for quantitative and qualitative changes in the recruitment procedures for the secondary school, an entrance examination to the 'sixième' grade served the purpose of eliminating (on the grounds of their 'inaptitude') those to whom formerly paying secondary education was barred.[42]

Progressively, children of poor classes, whose aptitudes were presumed to be 'practical' rather than 'complex', found themselves in channels (technical colleges, short secondary cycle, modern section) which actually diminished their chances of educational progress and choice. Similarly, the sex discrimination, which had been suppressed in theory, was ultimately reintroduced through institutional channels which were conceived to cope with the various aptitudes; girls whose verbal aptitudes appeared 'scientifically established' were directed to sections in which modern languages were predominant, or to those in which a literary-type education was dispensed rather than to scientific or technical education, leading to a specific vocational training. Selection procedures for these different categories, which quickly proved effective, were operative up to the university level. However, it is obvious that within each specific social category, a more or less substantial minority shows an educational performance that may be judged acceptable, and sometimes even exceptional; but such statements of fact have not at all shaken the belief in an essential difference. On the contrary, this difference, put in absolute terms, has marked success as something specific of its own.[43] Educational success cannot offset the handicap which ties down members of specific social categories to specific aptitudes. Nothing can bridge the fundamental lack — which is presupposed and imposed. This is brought out by a dichotomous and hierarchical classification, the variable content of which is unimportant since the point is always to attribute value to the few at the expense of the many.[44]

The more or less conscious reference to an overall ideology of aptitudes somehow operates a necessary and efficient mediation in the educational selection process, by which an adjustment is produced between the 'wishes' of students and their families and established educational and occupational openings. There is no educational reform project,[45] no text or circular dealing with selection and educational guidance that does not refer explicitly to what seems glaringly obvious to reformers: aptitudes. Yet the term aptitude, which is in such current use today, has been given a non-ambiguous meaning; the same has happened to other words such as 'ability', which largely have the same connotations in spite of users' intentions to discard the essentialist conception which the word aptitude betrays. Commonsense definitions have been enriched by the findings of the new science of tests since scientific apprehension of individual or category differences has reinforced the new meaning of the word. Therefore, in dictionaries specific definitions have replaced the generalizing definitions of aptitude which had been usual before scientific researchers, among others, conferred on it the meaning of a definite, measurable, innate character, which tends to differentiate individuals.[46] The definition offered by the *Encyclopaedia Universalis*, published in 1968, is the following: 'Inborn factors of individual differentiations (aptitudes in the sense understood here)'. Robert,[47] which relies on Claparède's definition, states that 'the test method aims at determining the particular aptitudes of an individual.' Although the commonly accepted definition, 'natural disposition to something', always refers to the idea of nature, examples illustrating this definition now refer to the empirical research from which natural classification criteria such as sex are taken: 'boys have always a particular aptitude for getting familiar with notions of this kind' (Jules Romain).[48] Hence, in current language, the term 'aptitude' designates an inborn character, a natural, substantial, causal reality which irreversibly marks the practical behaviour of social actors. If all that is told and translated into words is at work in the unconscious mechanisms which rule self-apprehension as well as the apprehension of others, then all is told to and imposed on a child once the word 'aptitude' enables him or her to conceptualize the multiple experiences on which depend his or her career as a char-woman, school teacher, or surgeon.

The ideology of natural inequalities conceived and promoted by a social class at a time when it took economic, and later on political, power gradually turned into a scientific truth, borrowing from craniometry, then from anthropometry, biology, genetics, psychology, and sociology (the scientific practice of which it sometimes oriented), the elements enabling it to substantiate its assertions. And by this very means, it was able to impose itself upon all the social groups which believed in the values presiding over the birth of aptitude as an ideology: namely Progress and Science. It now appears that well beyond the controversies, which oppose the different established socio-political groups, this general ideology directs the whole conception of selection and educational guidance: the educational system aims at selecting and training an 'élite', which by its competence, merit, and aptitude, is destined for high functions, the responsibility of which entails certain social and economic advantages. For some authors the science of tests should contribute to ensuring the sound functioning of a society, founded on merit, of which M. Young has given an imaginative, though quite convincing, picture.[49] Others, holding that tests merely reflect a social system which they refuse to accept, nevertheless talk of 'aptitude' or 'abilities', which should allow the guidance of individuals in a future society freed from inequalities which are inherent in the capitalist society.[50] Generally speaking, the idea of a just and equitable selection ensured by institutions offering everybody equal opportunities to establish his or her 'true' aptitudes constitutes the bedrock of a conception which seeks to legitimize social order, founded on the value attributed to individuals who are ultimately regarded as fundamentally unequal.[51]

The nineteenth-century patterns of thought seem still to be prevalent in research in the social sciences. Owing to the scientific division of labour, the findings of social sciences have a fragmentary character, which is unlikely to eliminate the ignorance of the general dynamic process in which psychological and social dimensions are involved. In the field of psychology the separation between research in psychoanalysis and experimental psychology does not facilitate the integration of respective findings into a more general theory of action. In the field of anthropology, women are still given a supposedly natural status, as N. C. Mathieu has so well analysed.[52] As for research in sociology, Chapters 4 and 5 will show that it is not yet freed of the prenotions which it is trying to get rid of.

But before looking at the new theoretical forms which essentialist ideology has taken on today, it is important to understand its dynamic force in everyday life. Indeed, for every social agent, the ideological grid according to which he spontaneously interprets reality is different according to the place he occupies in the economic system. How does essentialist ideology mark everyday practices? It is through an analysis of the contents of the speech of students who have undergone scholastic selection that we will approach the problem.

Notes

1 The terms used here refer to T. Herbert's definitions; cf. his article 'Réflexions sur la situation théorique des sciences sociales et spécialement de la psychologie sociale', *Cahiers pour l'Analyse*, 1966, no. 2, pp. 174–203.

2 F. Brunot, *Histoire de la langue française, des origines à 1900*, vol. 1: *De l'Epoque latine à la Renaissance*, Paris, A. Colin, 1913.

3 Further readings checked, according to F. Brunot (op. cit.) and G. Matoré (*Histoire des dictionnaires français*, Paris, Larousse, 1968):
J. Nicot, *Thresor de la langue française tant ancienne que moderne*, 1606.
Vaugelas, *Remarques sur la langue française utiles à ceux qui veulent bien parler et bien écire*, 1647.
P. Bouhours, *Remarques nouvelles sur la langue française*, 1675.
Richelet, *Dictionnaire français contenant les mots et les matières et plusieurs nouvelles remarques sur la langue française . . .*, 1680.
Furetière, *Essais d'un dictionnaire universel contenant généralement tous les mots français tant vieux que modernes et les termes des sciences et des arts*, 1690.
Abbé Prévost, *Dictionnaire portatif des mots français dont la signification n'est pas familière à tout le monde*, 1750.
Dictionnaire de Trévoux, *Dictionnaire français et latin vulgairement appelé* Dictionnaire de Trévoux, 1771 (new revised and enlarged edition of Furetière).
Abbé Féraud, *Dictionnaire critique de la langue française*, 1787.

4 B. Groethuysen, *Origines de l'esprit bourgeois en France*, vol. 1: *L'Eglise et la bourgeoisie*, Paris, Gallimard, 1927.

5 According to Gall, there is a parallelism between the development of faculties and the development of the brain, but his research does not come under the idea of a biological determinism. It is

only in the course of the nineteenth century, as we shall see later on, that psychological and cultural phenomena were considered to be directly influenced by physical differentiae, and, *inter alia*, by the difference in brain volume; one may recall the success of phrenology during these days, which Flaubert reflected in his *Bouvard et Pécuchet* and the *Dictionnaire des idées reçues*.

6 After 1830, this class, to all intents and purposes, held political, economic and social power.

7 Letters sent from different parts of France to the Abbé Grégoire – a famous philanthropist whose writings had a great impact just before the Revolution.

8 Societies of different kinds which appeared spontaneously all over the country, in which everyone could freely express his criticisms and suggestions.

9 F. Brunot, op. cit., vol. 4: *La Révolution et l'Empire*. The expression has not the same meaning here as it was to have in the nineteenth century. It designated all those who 'work with their hands', salaried workers, as well as self-employed craftsmen.

10 De Wailly, *Nouveau Dictionnaire français ou abrégé du dictionnaire de l'Académie*, Paris, An 9 (1801).

11 Quoted by F. Brunot, op. cit., vol. 4, part 2, ch. XII.

12 Ch. Morazé, *Les Bourgeois conquérants–XIXe siècle*, Paris, A. Colin, 1957.

13 Cf. for the history of education after this period, A. Prost, *L'Enseignement en France 1800–1967*, Paris, A. Colin, 1968.

14 Did any of the others want to enter the legal profession, for example? 'Without money, protectors, talent or the patience necessary to emerge from obscurity, one is doomed to failure'; such was the prediction of the forerunners of present career consultants who wanted to 'cope with an urgently felt need by providing an overview of the various job opportunities which are available to the intelligence and activity of man, with a summary indication of the aptitudes which are required and particularly of the conditions of time, instruction and money . . .', *Instructions pour le peuple. Cent traités sur les connaissances les plus indispensables*, Paris, 1850.

15 M. Parchappe, *Histoire physique de l'homme*, Paris, 1849.

16 Towards the middle of the century, Gobineau was to write referring to ancient Greece: 'At that time, one talked of slaves in much the same tone as one talks today of workers and proletarians', A. de Gobineau, *Essai sur l'inégalité des races humaines*, Paris, P. Belfond, 1967 (First edition: 1852).

17 J. Ch. Laveaux, *Dictionnaire synonymique de la langue française*, Paris, 1826. The pejorative tone prevalent before the Revolution turns up again here.

18 F. Galton, *Hereditary Genius–Its Laws and Consequences*, London, Macmillan, 1869.

19 One of the items on Terman's intelligence test, which is still used,

consists in summing up a paragraph like this: 'if we are able to sort out the influence of heredity as distinct from that of environment, we might well be in a position to use our science for the orientation of human development at large'.

20 In his early work, Binet used to regard the anatomical method (craniometry, measurement of body development, identification and interpretation of stigmata of degeneracy, etc.) as one of the methods of exploring intelligence. Cf. A. Binet, 'Le développement de l'intelligence chez les enfants', *L'Année psychologique*, vol. 14, 1908, pp. 1–94.

21 E. Durkheim, *On the Division of Labour in Society*, London, Macmillan, 1933 (French edition 1893). However, although he holds that 'the more specialized the forms of activity get, the further they are from the impact of heredity' (the laws of which in his opinion 'immutably govern the distribution of aptitudes' in the societies of castes), Durkheim still clings to the mental categories of his time by his belief that heredity actually does transmit 'very general abilities'.

22 A. Binet, op. cit.

23 A. Binet, 'Nouvelles recherches sur la mesure du niveau intellectuel chez les enfants d'école', *L'Année psychologique,* vol. 17, no. 6, 1911, pp. 145–201.

24 E. Littré, *Dictionnaire de la langue française*, Paris, Hachette, 1883.

25 This interest is explained by the practical difficulties which arose out of the implementation of compulsory education.

26 A. Binet, 'A propos de la mesure de l'intelligence', *L'Année psychologique,* vol. 12, no. 7, 1905, pp. 113–36.

27 Thus, 'tapping' tests are considered essential for judging clerical aptitudes, 'executive' vocational selection tests lay emphasis on a 'rich fount' of personality (commanding aptitude etc.); whereas the guiding selection principle for a typist will always focus on typing speed.

28 While discussing publications by American sociologists relating to educational inequalities, J. C. Combessie emphasizes an analogous error common to most writers; while referring to the 'value' concept as an explanatory principle of behaviour, they offer but a negative definition of the value system of the 'lower classes'. Cf. 'Education et valeurs de classe dans la sociologie américaine', *Revue Française de Sociologie*, vol. 10, no. 1, 1969, pp. 12–36.

29 G. Canguilhem indicated the scientific, political, technological, and economic conditions which weighed heavily upon the creation of a branch of psychology as the 'science of reactions and behaviour', and which oriented research toward aptitudes and their basic assumptions. Cf. 'The concepts of aptitude and capacity: the elaboration of concepts and methods of differential psychology in the 19th and early 20th centuries', in 'Qu'est-ce que la psychologie?', *Cahiers pour l'analyse*, no. 2, March 1966 (reproduction of a talk given in 1956). Cf. also more recently L. S. Hearnshaw, *XIIe*

Congrès International d'Histoire des Sciences; Colloques, Textes des Rapports, ed. A. Michel, 1968.

30 The list of aptitudes lengthens impressively, e.g. the *Dictionary of Education* lists the following: academic, artistic, educational, language, learning, mechanical, music, phonetic, reading, scholastic, social, special vocational. *Dictionary of Education,* V. Carter, New York, Toronto, London, 1958. This enumeration is far from being the longest or most detailed.

31 E. Claparède, *Comment diagnostiquer les aptitudes des écoliers,* Flammarion, 1924. Cf. ch. III, p. 29: 'Les aptitudes et leur structure'.

32 H. Piéron, *Traité de psychologie appliquée,* Paris, PUF, 1949.

33 H. Piéron, *Vocabulaire de la psychologie,* Paris, PUF, 1953.

34 C. Burt, 'L'Hérédité de l'aptitude mentale', in *Le Travail Humain,* XXIème année, nos. 1–2, 1958.

35 P. Naville, *Théorie de l'orientation professionnelle,* Paris, Gallimard, 1945.

36 M. Reuchlin, *Traité de Psychologie appliquée,* vol. III, Chapter 2: 'Le problème théorique de la connaissance des aptitudes', Paris, PUF, 1949.

37 In this respect, methodological refinements and careful analysis are interesting, since they reveal the prevalent hierarchy of the psychological 'dimensions'.

38 It could be objected that such an analysis belongs to other disciplines; but is the present compartmentalization of knowledge and research pertinent to the question?

39 Thus, the wish formulated by Binet in his early days, when working on metrical intelligence scale, may materialize: 'When the work, which is only outlined here, has taken a more definite character, it will doubtlessly enable psychologists to resolve a lot of problems, since what is at stake is the measurement of intelligence; thus, it will be possible to measure differences in intellectual level not only by age, but also by sex, social conditions, race, etc.; application of our methods may be made to ordinary, as well as to criminal, anthropology', 'A propos de la mesure de l'intelligence', *L'Année psychologique,* vol. 1, no. 7, 1905, pp. 113–36.

40 C. Guillaumin, *L'idéologie raciste. Genèse et langage actuel,* Paris, Mouton, 1971.

41 This concern has led to the establishment of so-called non-verbal tests (used, *inter alia,* in a French large-scale enquiry undertaken by the Institut National d'Études Démographiques, *Le Niveau intellectuel des enfants d'âge scolaire,* Paris, PUF, vol. I, 1950, vol. II, 1954. This, however, presupposes that the world of signs other than words (drawings, pictures, gestures etc.) is an immediate, universal, and natural datum which has nothing to do with the mastering of a linguistic code, or actual experience on which symbolic representations are founded.

42 This examination, set up in 1933, when free secondary education

was established, started to serve its screening purpose effectively only after the Second World War.

43 That is what R. Tchidimbo noted: 'Les étudiants noirs parlent', *Présence Africaine*, 1953, no. 14: 'If the African student succeeds in his studies, this is simply because he can call on an excellent memory.' Children of 'poor' classes are generally recognized as having the same 'advantage', since it is nothing but a compensation for a lack of more appreciated aptitudes. (Flaubert already noted in his *Dictionnaire des idées reçues ou Catalogue des opinions chics*: 'Memory: to complain about one's own or even to boast of not having any; but to get angry when you are told you lack judgement.')

44 Since the nineteenth century, there have been many examples of this classification procedure, which illustrate the impact of the dominant ideology on research in aptitude for social science. For A. de Gobineau, 'imitation' is unlikely to be a substitute for 'an indefinite intellectual development' (op. cit.). For A. Binet, the 'learning faculty' has nothing in common with the 'intellectual faculty'. The essential question is for E. Claparède: 'Does a given child show a better performance than others simply because he concentrates more or because he really is specifically gifted?' (op. cit.).

45 L. Decaunes et M. L. Cavalier, *Réformes et projets de réforme de l'enseignement français de la Révolution à nos jours (1789–1960)*, Paris, Institut Pédagogique National, 1962.

46 It should be recalled that the specification which appeared in the eighteenth century related to the area of a disposition which was held to be contingent: 'One is said to have an aptitude for science . . .' This specification now refers to individual or social categories.

47 P. Robert, *Dictionnaire alphabétique et analogique de la langue française*, Paris, Société du Nouveau Littré, Dictionnaire Le Robert, 1953.

48 *Larousse du XXe siècle*, Paris, Librairie Larousse, 1961.

49 M. Young, *The Rise of Meritocracy 1870–2033. An Essay on Education and Equality*, London, Thames & Hudson, 1958.

50 Cf. in this respect the critical analysis by L. Sève in 'Pour un développement créateur du marxisme', *Cahiers du Communisme*, nos. 5–6, May–June 1966: Débats sur les problèmes idéologiques et culturels (pp. 89–92). This criticism refers to a passage of a draft resolution of the French Communist Party stipulating that Democratic Education should 'ensure the promotion of each on the basis of his aptitudes'. In the final project, the word 'capacity' was substituted for 'aptitude', but we already pointed out that the common language connotations of both terms are identical.

51 A. Jensen and Hans J. Eysenck recently became the new spokesmen of this view in the field of psychology.

52 N. C. Mathieu, 'Homme-culture et femme-nature?', *L'Homme*, vol. 13, no. 3, 1973, pp. 101–13; 'Notes towards a definition of Sex

Categories', *The Human Context*, vol. 6, no. 2, 1974, pp. 345–61, and, *International Journal of Sociology*, Winter 1975–6, vol. V, no. 4, pp. 14–38; 'Paternité biologique, maternité sociale . . .', in *Femmes, sexisme, sociétés*, A. Michel (ed.), Paris, PUF, 1977, pp. 39–48.

2 The ideology at work in everyday speech. The rationalization of school choices

The social agents involved in the class system interpret the possession or deprivation of knowledge and power in all its forms according to the irrational logic that dominant ideology imposes on each person, whatever his/her position in the system of dominance relations. Far from being perceived as the result of socio-historic forces, social inequalities are attributed to a dynamic principle which existed before them and independently of them, to a so-called natural force. This obscure force is conceived of as an interior and immanent necessity, as the only creator of social reality, as we have seen in Chapter 1.

In which way is this ideology marked in the experienced and imaginary relationships of the social agents with their own practices? One can look for the answer to this question by comparing the objective factors (class, sex, etc.) determining the behaviour of students with the way in which they express their views on the history of their school and occupational life. Whereas statistical regularities show that school choices are socially imposed on each group and each individual according to his/her position in the economic system, as will be seen, students tend to reinterpret their school history in terms of aptitudes, of individual choices, and not in terms of social determinations. In fact, for school selection to work efficiently to the benefit of the dominant group, it is important that each individual unconsciously adjusts his/her behaviour so as to not perturb the school system. And this submission to the demands of the system can only work through a failure to recognize the dominance relationships present in selection.

The antagonisms which are expressed and reinforced at school could not lead to an objective hierarchy of social status without the existence of a series of symbolic mediations. First, a mediation in temporal horizons, since any behaviour is the actualization of a project, i.e. a projection into the future of a social 'me' defined here and now by the set of its sociological determinations. Thus an analysis of the differential relationship to time according to the social groups leads one to specify what is marked, the apprehension of their identity by social agents. But what of this identity? Can they answer the question 'Who am I?'

outside the definition of themselves imposed by dominant discourse?

Deprivation and possession of economic power and the power of knowledge

In 1974, we published a study of the selection processes at university, under the title *Les Inéqaux ou la sélection universitaire.*[1] We summarized some of the results of a first study which relied on school files. Out of a population of 6,919 Parisian students enrolled in the first-year course in *Lettres* in 1962,[2] 50 per cent failed the end of year exam (half the population consisted of dominant-class children). Economic factors partly explain these results: 57 per cent of the students originating from the dominated class had a full-time job (as teachers, boarding-school masters, etc.); only 17 per cent of the students originating from the dominant class were in the same position. And the chances of obtaining a diploma were twice as high for students who were not obliged to earn a living.

Eight years later, in 1970, we did a survey by correspondence to find out what the 3,242 students who had failed the exam had become from a scholastic and occupational point of view. The results have led to the following conclusions: at each stage in the educational curriculum, the degree of openness of the field of possibilities is a function of both the individual's social class origin and sex category. What happens to students from the dominated class and women (whatever their class) is based on this reality: to be a woman or a worker is to be dominated on the economic level and to lack the means of acquiring the necessary knowledge to exercise power in its various forms. We will first present the objective characteristics of the school and occupational histories of this surveyed population before analysing the speech of students who reinterpreted their own histories; it is the confrontation of these two realities which is relevant.

The students' family characteristics in the sample conformed to those of the general French population.[3] The fathers and mothers of students from the dominated class had rarely reached more than the *certificat d'études primaires* (a certificate at the end of primary school), whereas the fathers of the students from the dominant class generally held a *diplôme d'études supérieures* (a degree in higher education), though their mothers had at most reached the level of the *brevet* (a certificate given in the middle of secondary school). In general, mothers who had, or had had, a job held a position in the occupational hierarchy which was either equal or inferior to that of fathers, but nearly half the mothers of students from the dominated class and three-quarters of those from the dominant class were in a situation of complete economic dependence, since they had no paid employment.

Two things are important in understanding what follows: first, that the majority of mothers in fact occupied a decentred position within their class; and second, that when we speak here of the dominated class it must not be forgotten that we are in fact dealing with a privileged and very limited section of this class. Various conditions must be simultaneously fulfilled for certain children to find themselves entering university. The particular sociological characteristics of the families of these students indicate their marginal position within the dominated class. For example, in 43 per cent of cases one member at least of the extended family had had some higher education; while certain distributions were particularly atypical for the class, viz. birth control and incidence of employment of married women with children. Various conditions were thus united, suggesting that economic and intellectual constraints were relatively less heavy for these families than for families in the dominated class as a whole. Doubtless the children owed their ability to undertake and succeed in secondary studies, and at least to attempt more advanced studies, to this relative liberation, unlike the majority of children of their class (who are early destined to paid employment).

The school history of the different categories of students throws light on the processes of segregation which are permitted by the hierarchical organization of the educational system. Very early on children of the dominated class are subjected to educational orientations which little by little restrict their range of final choices. Though they may be marginal within their class, dominated-class parents still have a position within the economic system which gives rise to constraints whose impact is felt in the children's educational progress. Economic constraints initially require that they choose the least costly educational establishments: *écoles communales* (State primary schools), *collèges d'enseignement général*,[4] and *écoles normales d'instituteurs*.[5] Dominant-class children are to be found much more frequently in private schools. In addition, students from the dominated class cannot undertake secondary schooling without causing material and financial problems to their families. Such financial difficulties are necessarily a part of everyday experience throughout the whole period of education:

'There was no one left to help on the farm. I'm an only child.' (While she was in higher education her father was sick and her mother worked in an aircraft factory, so that the student herself had to give them financial help.)

'Free schooling at the *école normale*. A contract with National Education Ministry signed at the age of 15!'

35

'After all, the *école normale* enabled me to manage and took the load off my parents.'

'The CEGs are the very organizations open to people without much money.'

But the types of knowledge transmitted in these different establishments and what these imply in terms of a limitation or non-limitation in subsequent choices in itself constitutes a fact of dominance:

'I never learnt a second language in the CEG because it wasn't done at that time, so I learned Italian all by myself.' (Woman student reading English – a second language is required for the CAPES, an exam enabling one to become a secondary-school teacher.)

'I could never have gone in for a degree in history because there are Latin tests, and I wasn't able to learn Latin by myself.' (Woman studying geography.)

Consequently, directions in higher education are predetermined, on the one hand, by gaps in the basic education previously received, and on the other, continuing economic constraints (80 per cent of dominated-class students worked the whole time they were studying). The great majority of dominant-class children have no material worries, however, and in order 'to keep as many strings to [their] bow for as long as possible', as one of them said, they often enrol for other courses in addition to the first year in *Lettres*. What is more, though the number of children in the family may be limited for students from the dominated class, going to university can only be afforded for one member of the family. It is not uncommon for brothers and sisters to contribute financially to the studies of one member of the family: e.g. the son of an agricultural worker said he owed his presence at the university to the help of his brothers and sisters, themselves agricultural workers, a char-woman and a clerk in commerce. On the other hand, in three-quarters of the families of the dominant class all, or the great majority, of the children had some higher education (as for example the children of one family: *École Polytechnique, Hautes Études Commerciales pour Jeunes Filles, Institut National Agronomique* (two of them), *diplôme d'études supérieures* in law, medicine, and philosophy).

The processes of differentiation and segregation are analogous for women of the dominant class. These students received a secondary-school education which restricts the number of possible future directions. It is true that they may have studied Latin and Greek (*classique*) unlike the women and men from the dominated class, but on entering the first form in the secondary school (sixth) the majority of them are directed towards Section B, which is less promising than Sections A and

C, chosen by boys. Possibilities are closed or open from very early on because certain models have been imposed since primary school. In the class where living conditions and level of education enable parents to help children with their school work, mothers usually help with French and fathers with Science and Mathematics. In higher education *Lettres* is in fact the only path offered to women. Some regret being driven to this choice:

> 'I should have entered *Seconde* C to go on to more advanced studies in the natural sciences.'

While it is a last resort for men from the dominant class, studying *Lettres* is the only ambition fostered by the parents of other categories of students. Very few dominated-class parents hope that their child will do any higher studies other than *Lettres* while most dominant-class parents have other hopes at least for their sons. In practice, the parents' wishes are not without influence:

> 'During my year of *philo* I always talked of doing *Lettres*, but I have decided to study Law instead. But my father made me enrol for *Lettres*.' (Daughter of a tax inspector.)

Differentiations between categories are again accentuated when studying *Lettres* has been given up. For the dominated-class children it generally involves a pure and simple renunciation of any plans for higher education and a final decision to get a job. Only dominant-class children benefit from the privilege of being able to change the orientation of their studies (in the sample as a whole, those who went on to undertake higher studies, viz. the majority of dominant-class boys, were mostly directed towards legal and commercial courses). Nevertheless, the channels of direction again differentiate men and women: not only do women of each class more often give up any further courses, but an important section of those who do persevere (and this applies particularly to women students of the dominant class, as we shall see) do not choose higher education but a short vocational training (secretarial or library schools, parapsychological studies such as occupational therapy, or paramedical studies such as physiotherapy, etc.).

The system of privation/possession oppositions is found again in the future occupations of each category. Eight years after enrolling in *Lettres* (i.e. in 1970) some students were still engaged in a course of study. It was above all the sons of the dominant class who benefited from the privilege of such long studies. Apart from these aged students, all the men and the majority of the women in the sample had entered employment. There were few women who had never had a job. The few who were not working in 1970 had stopped working at the birth of children and generally considered this interruption to be temporary.

None the less, at the time of the survey, a quarter of the women were in a situation of total economic dependence for an indefinite period.

An evaluation of the occupation levels achieved (in the current or last job) shows sharp divisions between the categories. The level attained was average in the sample as a whole — except for dominant-class boys, of whom 75 per cent held posts high up in the occupational hierarchy. Of course, they more often had a *diplôme d'études supérieures*, but the possession or the lack of such a diploma is not sufficient to account for the disparities. A third of the dominant-class boys who had no *diplôme d'études supérieures* whatsoever had a high status in the hierarchy. (Only a few men from the dominated class and a minority of women from the dominant class had an equivalent hierarchical status when lacking such a *diplôme*.) Conversely, almost all the dominated-class women who finally got a *diplôme d'études supérieures* (and this, it will be recalled, was a tiny minority) became middle management and not higher ranking staff.

The income hierarchy is a result of all the orientations which have operated since the first day at school as a constant factor of differentiation. Dominant-class boys had the highest incomes and women from the dominated class had the lowest. In all, men came out ahead, followed by women, and differences within each sex category occurred according to social class origins. Thus the income of men with dominated-class origins was close to that of women from the dominant class (although these women more often had a *diplôme d'études supérieures*). These differences in income cannot be explained solely in terms of differences in levels of education since they are evident even when the diplomas were equal. It is striking that categories which are both dominant and dominated (i.e. men from the dominated class and women from the dominant class) arrived at roughly the same point: their occupational and income levels were similar (though we should not lose sight of the fact that a third of the women who came from the dominant class had no occupational income whatever). Of course their social status was not the same. Dominated-class children of both sexes situated themselves in 'threshold' categories (lower middle class). Their spouses came from the same class as they did and generally had the same type of occupation. On the other hand, 85 per cent of the women born in the dominant class had married men of a higher socio-occupational level, and the majority of the women themselves were either middle-management workers, or 'not working'. But is it logical to define these women's class identity by equating them with their spouses? Like their mothers, they had come to occupy a marginal position within the dominant class.

The male and female students from the dominant class have thus remained in their class, but with the women occupying a decentred position. Due to the particular situation of their families, the dominated-class students have been able to acquire the knowledge and *savoir-faire* which allows them to be socially less at a loss than their parents and kin. Having escaped certain forms of constraint which are inherent in the position of the dominated class, they have put themselves in categories which, while objectively dominated, are themselves the necessary machinery for the transmission and exercise of the dominant class's power: teachers judge the educational performance of dominated-class children; they embody the law in the eyes of that class; they are invested with the power given by knowledge. However clearly they may see the processes of selection in which they are involved, it is their collective activities that form part of the functioning on which the education system rests. Among the students from the dominated class, women ran up against the constraining social imperatives more than men, and, hence, had not been able (unlike some of their masculine homologues) to reach a high level in the occupational hierarchy. But despite this, the disparities between the socio-occupational futures of men and women students from the dominated class were less prominent than between men and women of the dominant class.

The system of oppositions between categories can be defined as relations of privation/possession — first at the level of acquisition of efficient knowledge, and then at the level of socio-economic future after schooling. Differentiation, segregation and selection do not take place by chance because the structure of oppositions and equivalents is the same at the finish as it was at the start. Meanwhile the problem is to establish by what mediations the relations of economic dominance bend the channels of differential orientation. At the first level of analysis it seems that the split between the categories could be thus explained: their position in the economic system implies a differential relation to time which can be seen in the continuity or discontinuity of their school and occupational history.

Open or closed temporal horizon

The relationship to time is not only a reflection or even an internalization of the undergone or exerted facts of domination, but rather a constitutive element in the situation of dominants and dominated, imposed by their objective position in the system of dominance. The dominants' position gives them hold over the future and enables them to make long-term plans. On the other hand, a system of constraints encloses the dominated in a present from which they cannot take their distance and which compels them to make short-term plans and to make one-way choices. The relationship to time is thus one of possession for some and of privation for the others. How far can the fact that temporal horizons are open or shut explain the continuity of the dominants, and the stops and ruptures which mark the educational and occupational history of the dominated?

The dominated class does not master time. Its temporal horizon is blocked both in the past and in the future. In the past, knowledge of the family background is limited to at the most two generations. The notion of ancestry only evokes the image of an obscure and nameless crowd, a crowd deprived of a class history since 'history' learned at school is that of the dominants. The dominant class, on the other hand, not only has a collective history which is transmitted, learned and known by everybody, it also has the histories of particular families, with genealogies. They have forefathers situated in time and space whose actions have marked the family annals, especially when a social ascent began. These genealogies are necessarily selective and are in fact only one of the symbolic expressions of one class's dominance. Open upstream, the temporal horizon of the dominant class is also open downstream: economic security and knowledge of the functioning of the education system allows long-term plans to be formulated for the children, as well as educational careers leading to the higher education level. For these children their period of education is continuous, and has no gaps; there are no stops or breakings off. Even in the event of failure, an eye is kept on the future:

> 'What I always wanted to do was cinema and anthropology together', said a student when he came back from his military service. (This was after he had repeated his first year of university and had already tried successively philosophy, theatre studies, art history, sociology and anthropology.)

However, time is not given as profusely to children of the female gender as to those of male gender, as we shall see. Only for the latter will the family invest a not inconsiderable portion of its capital, often over many years. The first objective is often to be as sure as possible of getting a diploma which will open up promising occupation prospects (although for many of them the future occupation is not necessarily out of reach without the diploma).

> Son of a university lecturer: he was preparing for the entrance exam to the *Ecole Nationale d'Administration* eight years after he first enrolled in *Lettres* (which followed three years in the first year) and after having spent two years in a private school.

> Son of a president director general: eight years after failing the exam at the end of the first year of *Lettres*, he was attending a course at the INSEAD (a prestigious private business school). He had previously tried without success to prepare the entry examination for the *Ecole*

des Hautes Etudes Commerciales and then for the *Ecole Supérieure de Commerce de Paris* (private).

Son of a polytechnician engineer: he had failed at the *Ecole des Hautes Etudes Commerciales*, then at the *Institut de Psychologie*. He went on to take a teaching post in a school for specialized educators. He was 'chief instructor' at the time of the survey (his salary was in the highest section relative to the sample as a whole) and he envisaged getting a post as director of the centre.

Son of an international civil servant: after having tried unsuccessfully to study psychology, he trained in a bank and thought that in a few years he would have the post of manager.

Thus there are no economic constraints to fix temporal boundaries to the future prospects of the sons of the dominant class.

In contrast, the constraining character of the situation in which the children from the dominated class live binds them to the present. Their relationship to the future is day to day. At the start their plans (based on a fundamental uncertainty as to the future and a lack of knowledge of the educational system) limit them to the *certificat d'études primaires* (primary school certificate), which most of them obtain. Secondary studies are just not thought of. This is the first dilemma, the first detour before the late entry into a secondary establishment of 'short cycle' for which their social class designates them. If they make up their mind to go on to the *baccalauréat*, at the end of the *troisième*, the need to take some insurance for the future leads them to choose a vocational channel, the *écoles normales*, to become a primary-school teacher. The entrance examination for this type of establishment often imposes a stagnating at the *troisième* level:

'Via the *lycées* I could have saved at least a year.'

'I had passed the BEPC the previous year and then the year afterwards I did a sort of *troisième*, a new *troisième*, a special *troisième*. Through this, I lost a year before entering the *école normale d'instituteurs*.'

In addition to these tramplings, the interruptions caused by immediate economic constraints (occupational commitment and/or the illness or lack of one parent) sometimes mark the development of the educational career:

'At the end of my *première* my father fell ill; I had no further resources, so I had to work.'

The *baccalauréat* is thus the limit set to studies:

'Of course, for my parents, the fact that I had the *bac* meant I had reached the peak. Having the *bac* was the end of the road. It meant something; the *école normale* was the end.'

Finally it was only after one or two years in an obligatory vocational training at the *école normale* for primary-school teachers that going to university became a possibility. Unlike the children of the dominant class, the presence at a university of a dominated-class child is but the realization of a plan which could only crystallize when doubts as to the upshot of the secondary studies were lifted. Before the higher courses, the educational career of dominated-class children presents a discontinuous, broken up character. They have certainly escaped some of the constraints imposed on the majority of children of that class (a schooling even more restricted in length and cultural content) but their course of study soon reaches its end.

At the time of higher studies the uncertain relationship to the future, based on economic constraints, continues to weigh on the orientations. It is not that their career plans must be less precise than those of dominant-class children, quite the reverse. For the latter:

'The aim (of higher education) didn't need to be known for it to be undertaken.' (Son of a telecommunications engineer: all four children of this father had diplomas from the *grandes écoles*[6].)

On the contrary, everything contributes to force dominated-class children into an extremely set choice: teaching. But the contradiction between the content of this plan and its relationship to the studies undertaken gives an idea of the uncertainty of the undertaking's results. Whereas the dominant-class boys expect, as they say, 'to have a high-level job' and 'to have important responsibilities', and while they consider further study to be indispensable, dominated-class children – whose aim is not so much to join the dominant class as to escape from the dominated class ('not to be a labourer', as the son of a skilled railway worker said) – generally come to consider higher education as 'important' rather than 'indispensable'. The plans of the former, supported by a family history, a class history, are collective plans. The majority of parents attribute great importance to their children's studies at university. The plans of the latter, in contrast, have an individual character. To get a *baccalauréat* is to reach the heights of the family's implicit aspirations.

'My parents didn't want to see me end on an assembly line or be a pen-pusher in the service sector.' (Son of a clerk.)

In addition only a minority of dominated-class parents attribute great importance to university success. The majority regard their children's schooling from afar and often with indifference. They are no longer directly involved at this stage, unlike the dominant-class parents.

When they enrol at the university, dominated-class children are older (over twenty) than dominant-class students because of their disjointed educational background and the interruptions in their studies after the *baccalauréat*. In addition, their age does not have the same sociological meaning within their class as it has within the dominant class, given the age differences by social class at the time of employment. If time can be frittered away by some children of the privileged, it must necessarily be saved by dominated-class children who need to go 'as fast as possible':

> 'After the *troisième*, I entered the *seconde technique*. Although my parents weren't opposed to my carrying on studying, I wanted to save time.'

> 'If I could start again, I would begin at 17. It's easier at 17 than at 22–3.' (He worked before starting his studies at the university at 22.)

But for most of them the future is already blocked and the break seems definitive. They are locked in a present whose constraints are too imperative not to be taken into account in the formulation of their plans: 'I thought about it [a degree] without believing in it.' Boarding-school masters, teachers or soon to become so, their aim is to 'progress', to 'improve' an occupational position which already assigns them a special social situation. They cannot see themselves primarily as students. Their presence at the university means a last attempt to open up the field of possibilities, but they are already out of the game. Their ephemeral passage through university marks the limits of their time in the educational system and, in fact, the point of no return.

The same processes are at work in the options of dominant-class girls. This category should, according to the norms of its class (which have been changing at the same time as the proportion of women has been increasing in the student population), reach the university after a smooth period of secondary schooling. But during their higher education, whilst the field of possibilities is getting restricted, their temporal horizons are blocked like those of dominated-class children. In the same way as at the age of twenty the relations to the past and the future cannot be identical for the student son of a worker and the student son of a higher executive, so to be twenty does not have the same sociological meaning for a man as it does for a woman. There is a strong chance that the social status of a woman will crystallize more rapidly than that of a man, given the difference in age at marriage.

If the future for dominated-class women students is partly closed as soon as they enter the university (they are teachers and will remain so), for women students of the dominant class this future takes on a hypothetical character as soon as they are involved in higher courses. From then onwards they are likely, given their age, to pass from economic dependence on their parents to dependence on a future spouse. Although women students of the dominated class have a job while studying, they are certainly aware that this occupational status may be in question when they marry, since women are responsible for unpaid servicing and the renewal of the 'labour force'. It is also not surprising that interrupting courses should be even more frequent for them than for their male colleagues from the same social origins.

However, the relationship to education differentiates men and women from the dominant class much more radically than men and women from the dominated class. Although some dominant-class women students stressed that in their social circle it was unusual for a woman to have a higher education, they generally considered it 'normal' to do such studies. But the final result of these studies was not clear, as the uncertainty of their plans denotes:

'Eventually to get a job.'

'To have a job which would enable me to earn my living, should the need arise.' (The possibility of the need not arising did not exist for their male fellow students.)

Also, many of them (unlike the dominated-class girls) did not reply when asked if they considered having a higher education was 'essential, important, or not very important', or when they were asked what importance they attached to getting a degree.

Thus the same processes are at work here as for dominated-class children. Most of the dominant-class women are also at the university on deferment. Suspending courses, orienting themselves towards short vocational courses (secretarial, library, etc.), is again a behaviour based on the closing of the temporal field imposed on their sex category. Thus it appears as if the dominated have no more time for learning when they reach the age of higher education. They have reached the threshold, the point of inevitable rupture caused by the social imperatives which enclose them within the immediate present.

The relationship to the future, which is different at the time of higher education, is still different when (towards the age of thirty) they almost all have a job. The future is practically closed for the majority of both sexes of the dominated class and for the majority of women from the dominant class. They have come to form the middle management. They know they have little chance of promotion and that in five or ten years they will still be doing what they describe as 'the same thing'. On the other hand, half the dominant-class boys have a much broader horizon and are in more prestigious and better-paid employment. They are certain to rise up the occupational hierarchy and to occupy (if they don't already) managerial posts. Further, their relationship to time in their everyday life is different. When the future is open, work is described as 'varied', 'lively', 'interesting', 'creative', and 'responsible'; time is rich and plentiful. In subordinate posts the work is described as 'monotonous', 'routine', 'irksome', and 'needing no initiative'; time is empty. These same descriptions are applied to housework, where the succession of routine tasks leads to a breaking down of time. This again reinforces the division between job and domestic activities for the majority of married women who go out to work ('the perpetual race between school and home').

The forms of time thus act as mediating factors in the genesis of occupational choice. It is as if the social agents evaluate what is possible, taking implicit account of their position in the system of dominance, while working out what schemes they want to carry out in practice. The relationships to time which can be read in their plans thus seem to indicate a definition of their own identity by the social agents. But, as we shall see, this definition is directly provided for them by the social discourse. In this the dominated are the object of a specification in the name of an essential incompleteness, while the dominant are singularized and defined as the incarnation of achieved human nature.

Incompleteness and wholeness

If the relationship to time is the sign of an implicit evaluation by each category of its probable future in relation to the probable future of other categories, this supposes at least the identification of several social groups and the perception of a difference between them. But in so far as the definition of the groups and the relations they maintain are socially imposed, students do not define their identity in the same way according to whether they come from the dominated or the dominant class, and whether they are men or women. Children of the dominated class always announce in some way, right from the start, a social origin which seems to them to make sense of their history and of the speech which restores it:

'My parents were workers.'

'I'm from a very working-class background.'

'My family is very, very simple.'

'My father was an agricultural worker.'

'There are very few of us from the working class at the university.'

On the other hand, the comments of those from the dominant class about their social origins seek only to individualize them, not to define them in terms of class membership. They may eventually allude, in passing, to their class background, but only so as to explain a detail of their history:

'My father, whose work is advertising books, has a lot of contacts in literary circles, with editors, authors.'

'My father wanted me to go in for a mathematical discipline because he's in one himself.'

'I did *classique* because my father, being a Latin teacher, thought he could give me all possible initial advantages.'

Women, whatever their class of origin, define themselves as part of a category, unlike men:

'I think I shall have a less good job than my father (my mother doesn't work). Less good because, being a woman . . . .'

'A difficult exam for a woman . . . .'

'It's not really a job for a woman.'

'A housewife.'

'The mother of a family.'

'Good pay for a woman.'

On the other hand, men do not think of their masculine status. For example, although it was uncommon for a boy to be the only one in a family to have had higher education, he would unhesitatingly declare that it was normal to go to university among his circle. He would never qualify it by adding 'for a man'. As the social characteristics of the dominant never define their identity, they are not uttered. Only the dominated groups are named, specified; but 'woman', 'the worker', 'the Jew', 'the black' are banal utterances which are significant only in reference to what is never mentioned: an individual male, bourgeois, Christian, white, etc. The hidden referent has all the characteristics of the perfect dominant.

Spatialization
If the dominated, unlike the dominant, announce which category they belong to, it is because in social discourse the former are marginalized. They are thrown into a closed, limited world – as is expressed by a collection of spatial metaphors. Topologically the representatives of the dominated class are 'under':

'I don't want to sink back.'

'I wanted to rise in the world.'

'Pulling oneself up by one's bootstraps.'

They are 'trapped', 'hemmed in'. Those who, thanks to relatively favourable conditions, were able to have at least a secondary education consider that they have 'escaped'; that they are now 'distanced' from their class; that they have 'got out', 'clambered out' or 'jumped over the barriers'. If there is a closed area, this can only be by reference to an open space, without frontiers – which is the place of the dominant. But this place is not designated.

By the same logic, the universe of the dominated category of women is an equally closed, limited, circumscribed world. Women's and men's discourse assigns women a defined space – viz. 'home', 'family', 'domestic' – where they 'go round', 'stay within the four walls', 'become bogged down', lead a 'secluded' life, becoming 'limited', 'dull' and even 'cut off' and 'isolated' from the rest of the world. This symbolism of enclosure applies equally to domestic activities and to occupational activities where the dependent status is particularly marked. Secretaries, for instance, speak of themselves as being 'closed in', 'blocked', and 'confined'. The same general opening function filled for dominated-class children by education is filled for women by paid employment. By working 'away from home' or 'outside', it is possible to 'get out of the house' and to 'broaden one's horizons', to have 'an opening into the outside world' and be 'integrated into collective life', to 'develop fully'.[7] For their part, women of the dominated class are faced by the obstacle of a double marginalization due to their sex and their class.

The notions of enclosure, and of getting out and opening up which are their corollaries, are part of the same system of perception of the real. To be a worker or a woman is to be apart, secluded, far from the mythical centre where the bourgeois man is situated. But the place of the dominant is never designated. One never says of a man, for example, that he works 'outside'. In the dominant discourse topological classifications serve the ideological function of disguising the existence of concrete social relations of dominance by transmuting them into relations of a formal, geometrical character – i.e. by spatializing them. But this space itself, the sign of a reification of social reality, is not neutral: the dominant is always there as the implicit referent.

Biologization

If the dominated are marginalized it is because lack of power means lack of being. A dominated person is thought an incomplete being.

Dominated sex   We have seen that dominant discourse gives women a supposedly natural social status. For the students concerned, how can we explain the undeniable fact that the majority of women are to be found in literary and non-scientific areas, in devalorized sectors of activity, in positions where their status is low in the hierarchy? Those who did high-level courses in science (which are more highly valued than arts) give explanations which are clearly common sense:

> 'You know you choose that [*Lettres*] by elimination. If you don't have a scientific mind, if you're no good at maths and science, well you come down to *Lettres*.'

> 'You absolutely must do C [maths and science] because if you don't do maths you're more or less devalorized. Those who do B [languages], philo, are considered worthless.'

These orientations are precisely the 'normal' ones for women. As they are supposed to be no good at science, they are convinced of it:

> 'I've followed the normal line: a *bac* B, then philo. My English teacher knew at once in the *sixième* that I was gifted. Lots of subjects interested me, except maths. I really don't have the mental make-up to go in that direction.'

Certain qualities of intuition, and sensitivity, considered to arise from a specifically feminine nature, are also used to explain the occupational choices which are socially imposed, e.g. the teaching profession:

> 'Even so one must try and understand pupils: That's why I think it's a feminine vocation.'

But it is precisely these qualities which show a lack of the required aptitudes for the higher offices held by men of the dominant class; offices which it is said require 'research work', 'responsibility', 'creativeness', 'organization' and ability to 'produce original work'. Women are seen not as creators but as procreators. Their 'natural', biologically based, destiny is motherhood. They are thought only to be able truly to 'fulfil' themselves by having and raising their own children. If they do not have children, it is generally considered to be desirable if not necessary that they be employed. Being 'a housewife at home' is generally disparaged as possibly bad for the mental balance of the wife and for the adjustment of the couple. When not working (or deemed not to be) women are liable to abandon themselves to their natural frivolity and even immorality. Thus it is necessary to 'avoid idleness' and a 'trivial life' by 'giving her something to do', a job which will 'give her something to think about', since 'idleness is the mother of all vices'. This suspicion is shared by representatives of both sexes. When women have children, their jobs should be compatible with family life and preferably should stop altogether when the children are 'young'.

These are recently adopted conceptions, however, and are the system of justifying a state of affairs in which some women are thrown into sectors of activity and jobs which are low in the hierarchy, while the rest are pushed into the unpaid work of maintaining and renewing the labour force. This system has been strengthened in the twentieth century by the popular diffusion of educational precepts supposedly based on the discoveries of psychoanalysis. A current of thought which says that the mother's presence close to young children is essential for their 'good' affective development, has been spread since the Second World War – just when a minority of women were starting to occupy posts[8] traditionally held by men. Whereas the essential point lies in love relationships, regardless of the kinship or sex of the person who looks after the child, these relationships have come to be substantified in the person of the mother. The need for her presence close to young children occurs as a leitmotiv in the accounts analysed. The mother's presence is 'essential', 'necessary', 'irreplaceable', for the 'happiness', 'development', 'adjustment' of the children:

'A child needs its mother.'

'The mother is the only one really capable of raising her children. The first years are the determining ones.'

Whether women have jobs or not, they have clung even more closely to this new form of the dominant ideology since the only form of power which is recognized for them is that which they exercise over the most sociologically dependent category, i.e. children.

In fact, whatever its content, the dominant discourse accounts for women's condition by attributing to them a deep-seated incapacity. If they direct themselves towards *Lettres* it is because they have specific aptitudes and because they can only succeed educationally in ways adapted to a minor form of intelligence – more intuitive, less abstract.

Dominated class   And what of children from so-called 'deprived' backgrounds? Why do they come across educational difficulties from the start of their schooling? If we enumerate the qualities necessary for success we can already supply the elements of the implicit reply to this question. A child's educational success presupposes 'something' within his or her genetic inheritance, as the history of the word 'aptitude' has shown in Chapter 1. There is a rich terminology applied to this metaphysical principle: intelligence, aptitudes, capacities, possibilities, dispositions, facilities, intelligence quotient, mental structure, taste, interest, openmindedness, a critical mind, an enquiring mind, etc.

> 'You need personal abilities, you cannot make up for a lack of these.' (Dominated-class son.)

> 'Unfortunately, on the intellectual plane, my brother doesn't really have the disposition or the taste.' (A girl of the same class.)

> 'In the school where I was, there were boys who were still . . ., perhaps not at 16 but . . ., trying to get their *certificat d'études primaires*, though they obviously weren't very bright.' (Dominant class son talking of small farmers' sons.)

Intelligence (defined as a substantive characteristic) is necessary but not sufficient. Other psychic and moral qualities are needed — namely, personality, character, courage, will, a strong disposition, enthusiasm, application, seriousness, etc.

> 'I know lots of young workers who started courses . . ., or rather the children of workers, and who stopped, because they wanted to have some money [. . .] . It's all a question of character. Basically those succeed who want to succeed, who have the will to do something in life.' (Dominated-class daughter.)

> 'When a man of the people really wants to raise himself to the level of the élite, the bigger the difficulties, the higher he'll climb.' (Dominant-class son.)

Finally, you need a 'good family background' which knows how to encourage, support, induce, stimulate, frame, supervise, and which shows its availability, will, firmness, strictness, etc.

If some are convinced that 'only the least able stay as labourers' (dominant-class male student) or that 'the children of workers and peasants have often inherited less aptitude for study' (dominated-class male student), it is very rarely that anyone refers equally explicitly to the ideology of aptitudes. People don't say straight out that dominated-class children have fewer aptitudes — quite the opposite:

> 'I'm absolutely certain the opposite is the case.'

> 'Heavens, no.'

> 'Not on your life.'

> 'No, no, no, not at all.'

The denials and the repetitions seem to be symptoms: one must repress what one cannot consciously avow when one otherwise believes in the reality or the necessity of a 'democratization' of education in the name of an egalitarian system of values.

Although the justification system should, in the end, stay the same, the expression has taken on a more masked aspect since the population of secondary and higher education has objectively lost its homogeneous character and since the composition of the dominant class has changed. Taking account of these objective facts, the interpretation of social reality has renewed its form. As we shall see in Chapters 4 and 5, sociology has taken over from psychology and its theory of aptitudes in providing the dominant ideology with a new scientific prop. Background factors and 'cultural' differences are now used more and more in the universal discourse as the new principles explaining differences in educational achievement. That this concerns a simple shift in the essentialist view of social reality is shown by the remarks noted. Far from being defined in relation to the system of economic, political and social interactions, which alone give it an identity, the 'background' (often reduced to the family background) is considered as an entity. The cultural differences involved are in the end differences *sui generis*.

What do those who fail lack *culturally*? 'A way of expressing themselves', 'a critical mind', 'openness of mind', 'a taste for non-utilitarian culture', 'a theoretical mind', 'a conceptual mind', 'certain values'. They have 'concrete minds', 'they value material things too much', 'peasants are more practical – they have a relationship with nature – and don't feel the need to intellectualize problems'. All such elements are considered as absolute characteristics, as transcendent and independent of the relations of dominance on which they are based. If the background is neither 'open', 'curious', 'stimulating' and 'provident', nor 'aware of the need for qualifications' or concerned for the 'individuality of the subject', it is because it is deemed to be the carrier of biological and moral defects. This belief, which is sometimes expressed explicitly ('the defect of hereditary alcoholism'), may generally be interpreted like the reverse of the accounts given of 'good' families, those whose children succeed: 'a balanced and non-disturbing background', 'a reliable family', 'stable', 'quiet', 'harmonious', where there is a 'good atmosphere', 'serene and caring', a 'regulated life', where 'the family situation is clear', a 'healthy climate'. If we compare these sort of responses with those on the dangers of idleness for childless women we can see that they both connote the idea of the amoral nature of the dominated.

When one appeals to differences of aptitudes or cultural differences to explain educational inequalities, the vision of social reality is set and static:

'The material and *cultural* reasons are dreadful and almost insurmountable' (emphasized by the respondent).

On the other hand, as we have already seen in relation to the use of spatial metaphors, the dominated are only defined in universal discourse in a negative fashion with regards to the dominant. They are enclosed somewhere else, they are irreversibly lacking in something. In the end, if the dominated, unlike the dominant, always indicate in one way or another what category they belong to ('my parents were working class', 'for a woman'), it is because the social groups to which they belong, and only these, are socially designated as a species apart. That the one should be the object of a specification and the other of a singularization is not without importance to the way in which each individual is situated within his or her group and within the social universe.

The dividing up or unity of identity

In their lived and unconscious relationship to what they are socially (due to the fact of their precise situation in the system of dominance), the dominants and the dominated cannot define themselves outside of what is imposed by the dominant discourse. The definition of their identity in terms of completeness for the former and incompleteness for the latter, leads for the dominated to a dividing up of the self which for the dominants is unified.

The class and sex dominants
The minority of individuals who, because of their class and sex category, belong to the group which has economic, political and ideological power at its command, never doubt their capacities. It seems that male students from the dominant class have never questioned their aptitude for higher education. As one of them said:

'The question would have appeared out of place.'

It goes without saying, in their *milieu*, that one is born intelligent and that educational success is but the logical consequence of something very obvious. It may be said explicitly, or expressed more modestly:

'I wanted to do something interesting, taking account of my talents.'

'It would be presumptuous to say that I'm more intelligent than others . . .'

'I'd always thought of getting a degree.'

'In my family we've always tended to think that exams should be passed at the first attempt, and well.'

Their aptitudes are revealed early on and are altogether singular and exceptional, distinguishing them from the rest as a unique subject:

'I've always wanted to be a writer, even when I was quite young. I started to make up poems when I was 6 . . . I still write today.'

'I've always had the intention from a very early age – but really very early, when I was 2 or 3 – of going to the *Ecole Normale Supérieure* [a very prestigious *Grande Ecole*] . It's strange, but that's how it's been.'

'I chose Indian studies mainly out of interest, and a bit out of a whim.'

'At ten years old I already had a passion for politics.'

If a setback has been experienced, it has not produced a final break. On the contrary, it has often been the occasion for discovering and setting in motion other capacities:

'My failing the exam at the end of courses of *Institut des Sciences Politiques* stopped me doing some competitive entrance exams [for the Foreign Office] which in the end was no bad thing because it allowed me to take a long trip to Latin America which impressed me.' [He was thinking of becoming a journalist or a press agent.]

'Failing the first exam at the university stopped me aiming for the *agrégation d'histoire.*'[9] (This had led him to become the 'administrator of goods in his own firm'.)

While not ignoring the hierarchy of disciplines, according to which the sciences have greatest prestige, they interpret their presence in *Lettres* by the logic of an imperious realization of the self, the product of an inner call, of a passion:

'My father wanted me to go towards the mathematical disciplines and I wanted to do philosophy. He valued my continuing with maths, but, well, I didn't! Each time I changed direction it was because I *had* to.'

Failure does not make the dominants question the high ideas they have of themselves. When they consent to use the common reasons of 'laziness' and 'dilettantism' it is so as to remove blame from themselves. The bad organization of the educational system and the 'lack of interest of the subjects' are in the end the true culprits. Some of them even go so far as to see educational success as the 'sign of a lack of intellectual originality', as the director of an advertising agency put it, being himself a former unlucky student.

'Brilliant people are not successful. At the beginning of university studies, it's the nice girl, totally dull, who takes precisely no interest at all in what she does. You find the least interesting people in the

53

universities. They don't attract others, by an intense personal life or by interesting ideas.'

'Nothing could be nicer than to be unfit for higher education!'

Their histories (whose contingencies are in their eyes unaccounted for by class or sex) are the pursuit of personal freedom, of a surely 'innate' knowledge, about the functioning of the educational and social systems, since no influence seems to them to have weighed on their choice. How were they oriented at the secondary level? It was a 'personal choice', 'it was I who wanted it', they declare. Elsewhere, when asked if some particular circumstances had influenced the unfolding of their life, they never make any reference to resolutions of a sociological kind (unlike the children of both sexes of the dominated class, and girls from the dominant class, as we shall see). For them, their social future is but the fruit of their quite singular subjectivity which makes them remember striking events in their history:

'The death of my mother, my father's strong personality and his frequent absences.'

'The fact of having been an unwanted child.'

'The fact that I was raised in absolute fear of the devil and that I then had the courage to resist it.'

'The excitement due to adolescence and the proximity of a piece of paper and a pen.' (He was a writer at the time and living on a personal income.)

'My family background: university free-thinkers.'

'Chance, prudence, humour.'

'Everything. The face of my grandmother, a certain sunset . . . .'

For men of the dominant class there is no hiatus between what they have 'chosen' to be (their social self) and what they would have liked to be. Their imaginary self derives from nostalgia for an aristocratic way of life (not to be subject to the burden of lucrative needs) and also, of perfect singularity: 'idle rich', 'lazy poet', 'gentleman's life', 'not to have a job at all', poet, novelist, actor; or again astronomer, 'shipwrecked like Robinson Crusoe', racing pilot, composer, painter, writer, or 'witness of the world'. Pure expression of an inner energy, detached from all social contingency, this imaginary 'I' corresponds to an idealized self precisely because they consider setting this sort of creative capacity (whose richness is inexhaustible) to work in the job which they say they have freely chosen. ('J.-L. L. [his name] is in itself an impressive platform.') In the comparison of self/others by which the dominant defines his identity, it is his 'me' which is valued and central and coherent, harmonious, without hiatus. There is homogeneity between his social 'me' and the imaginary referent.

The dominated sex

The definition of their identity is not as obvious for women, whatever their class origin. Taking the dominant discourse into account, they think of themselves both collectively and singularly. Certainly, just as their masculine counterparts stay in the dominant class, women who are marginalized within this same class think they have chosen their direction quite freely. However, certain choices, experienced as free choices, question little by little their idea of an autonomous self; they are overwhelmed by the situation that they have 'chosen'. Marriage and maternity above all introduce a break in the unfolding of an educational or occupational history hitherto lineal and without jolts. Whether they see marriage and motherhood as losses or gains, for women it is always an event which introduces a discontinuity in their future:

'If I wasn't married I would have accepted a job needing a lot of moving about.'

'My husband was very keen for me to act as his collaborator.'

'My marriage and the birth of the first child . . ., afterwards things went very swiftly.'

'After the birth of the first child I couldn't work anymore and I had to follow my courses alone at home, which is why they were so seriously delayed.'

'I married very young which made me become a primary-school teacher after the *bac*. Then my children and my trip to the United States with my husband made me interrupt my work, then my divorce obliged me to work again before having finished my course.'

In alluding systematically to what they have experienced as particular circumstances, they are only expressing a condition which imposes channels on all those in their category.

These channels are also imposed on women from the dominated class — albeit the latter are far less likely to evoke marriage and the birth of children when asked if particular circumstances have influenced the unfolding of their life. As compared with women of the dominant class, their marriage has much less often been the occasion for interrupting a course or their occupational activities; but on the other hand, they did not have to wait for this event to notice that certain social constraints impose limitations on individual choices. They refer to the many and varied obstacles which they came up against over a long period because of their class origin, more often than they refer to marriage:

> 'When my father died I broke off my studies. Before that I'd chosen a job which would give financial help to my parents.'

> 'The financial position of my parents wasn't good; it is for that reason I chose *école normale d'instituteurs.*'

> 'My mother was sick, my father in a small job and a sister to bring up, hence the necessity to have paid employment and a few hours free to work.'

> 'Coming from a working-class family, my father wanted me to get a job after the *baccalauréat.*'

Their class origin is for them the explanation of what happens to them, but this does not imply that they do not make reference elsewhere to their marital status. We shall in fact see that they do not overlook the fact that marriage and the birth of children has introduced (or is in danger of introducing) changes in their present lives. Men, in contrast, whatever their class, rarely allude to that which objectively has not introduced any discontinuity to what happens to them. Their marriage and their family are absent from their field of discourse.

That women refer themselves to a system of social constraints does not mean that they are necessarily aware of the relations of dominance between the sexes. If they may wish to convince themselves of their freedom by speaking of their singular aptitudes in the way that the sons of the dominant do, they cannot at the same time avoid expressing by their words the restriction of this freedom:

> 'When I was young, I was good at English because it interested me.'

> 'One of the things which made me successful was that I liked what I was doing. Well I liked it. I loved English. I love it as a language and as a culture.'

The repetition doubtless fulfilled a reassuring function for the author of this account because she could not ignore the fact that the majority of women who are at university are devoted to *Lettres* and particularly to languages. In affirming that 'I was gifted at English and not at maths', 'Teaching was always my vocation', 'I love children', in exalting sensitivity, affection, the realization of oneself in motherhood, they all want to convince themselves of their singularity. But this attempt to give value to their 'me', whose limits are those assigned to their 'species', only leads to enclosing them within these same limits.

The necessity to value themselves as women is in fact only the expression of a knowledge that they share collectively; they know unconsciously that to be a woman is socially to be 'less'. In fact, the professional choices they dream of are far from being uniquely related to activities which are socially reserved for women. Although the imaginary choices of men concern exclusively activities which are in fact performed by men, there is a hiatus between what women have become (mainly primary-school teachers, secretaries, research assistants and 'housewives') and what they would often like to be (doctors, surgeons, lawyers, judges, anthropologists, architects, atomic energy researchers, politicians, ministers, etc.) — jobs all of which are really held by men from the dominant class. Of course, the influence of the social models which restrict the field of social activities of women can still be seen in their expressed wishes: obstetrics, gynaecology, pediatrics, children's judge and secondary-school teacher. However, the way in which they identify with the dominant is more open when they project onto their children (whatever their sex) the wishes which they cannot express directly. They want their children to realize themselves, to be creative, free and independent.

Of course, the replies are a little different according to the nature of the handicap which the women come up against owing to their social origins. Women from the dominated class whose projects for individual promotion were blocked said that they would have liked to be teachers (of literature, German, history, philosophy, etc.) more often than women from the dominant class. (The same remark can also be made in relation to men. The only men who express, and can express, a regret about not having been a secondary-school teacher are students from the dominated class, for this choice is for them, as for women, one of the possibilities of 'opening up' and it has been refused them.)

It was only because of their sex category that women from the dominant class could not realize some projects. One would have liked to have been a doctor, another a designer, but their parents opposed these orientations. Others followed specialized studies but without getting the desired occupation:

A married woman without a job who had actually followed a course in publishing and bookselling would have liked to run a bookshop.

A single woman with a degree from the *Ecole du Louvre* (art school), who wanted to be an archeologist, ended up as a filing clerk.

A married woman without a job, who failed at the *Institut des Sciences Politiques*, had wanted to be a minister.

Some of them stressed that it is because they were women that they ran up against particular social prohibitions. One wanted to go to a hotel and catering college but she knew 'there were no openings for women'. Another wanted to be an agricultural engineer but 'gave up because of [her] sex'. What they could not and cannot be in reality, they lived in their imaginary world. Certain slips are symptomatic of the division between their social 'self' and their unconscious 'I'. For example, in reply to the question: 'Sex: M or F?', several women had marked the first possibility (male), but no man made a mistake. Perhaps it is not so much the economic, legal or political power in itself that the category of women wish to share with the category of men, but rather the possibility (through this power) of asserting that they are social subjects, that they are incarnations of humanity and not a sub-species of humans.

If unconsciously the 'I' of women is that of the dominant (man of the dominant class) they do not in the meanwhile stop living the condition of a dominated, hence the split in their identity and the incoherence of their practices. The occupational activity of women is experienced as much, if not more, as a moral reality than as an economic reality. The idea of sacrifice is associated with it either in relation to children (if the mother works) or in relation to the mother (if she does not). Those who work transgress a social norm; those who do not work are closed in a dependent status and deprive themselves of the possibility of self-realization. Hence temporary or final stopping of occupational activity is accompanied by the wish to start work again, or women work while feeling guilty about their children. They show profound uncertainty about themselves, about their own wishes, and uncertainty about maternity (considered as an inevitability) and what is the right thing to do:

A teacher, married with two children: 'If I had another child I think I would take a holiday, or maybe I would go back to studying.' (Having wanted to do medicine, she said she was 'obliged to work' after her marriage in 1962 to a medical student, who himself carried on with his studies.)

A housewife with three children: 'I look after the children myself at the moment as they need me. I'm often stupified by doing the same things over and over again.' She said she had a 'nervous breakdown' and wanted to work.

A housewife with two children: After failing the exam to get into a pharmacy course, she married at twenty and then enrolled in university at a time when, she said, '[she] had no understanding of the interest of studying'. Then she took a job as a teacher. Eight years later she was no longer in this occupation, and did not wish to be in it. She would like to become a social psychologist and was thinking of taking up studying again.

A housewife with two children who had taught for a year in a secondary college (the succession of statements, given in the order in which they were produced, shows an unresolved conflict):

1 In reply to the question relating to occupation: 'char-woman, nurse, maid of all work, painter and decorator.'
2 She thinks it better 'for the happiness of the children' that the mother does not work.
3 What will she be in five years time: 'Nothing . . . i.e. a mother.'
4 Her situation, which produced 'intellectual boredom', seemed to her final but 'hope still lives'.
5 When asked to indicate what particular circumstances had influenced the unfolding of her life, she said: 'Early engagement, which took away from me all opportunities for occupational success because I wanted to bring up the children I intended to have.'
6 In reply to the question on occupational choices for children, she said that it is less necessary for girls to have a higher education.

Of course, although clear in these replies, the conflict experienced by non-working women is often masked. They must repress the desire for independence and to transgress the norm. Indeed, they do not really have the possibility of transgressing it. They thus project the actualization of these desires into a hypothetical future, with 'hope' but without illusions. They also have no other possibility than to reassert their attachment to the norm that the wife should not work if she has children. Very few of them thought, unreservedly, that it was preferable for both members of a couple to have a job. Women with jobs expressed this opinion a little more often, but the fact that it is still the opinion of the minority shows the weight of the dominant ideology. Even the replies of this minority (whose values system conforms to their practice) attest the existence of a conflict.

We have seen that men do not talk about either their marriage or fatherhood when thinking about the particular circumstances which have influenced their history. In the same way married men and fathers almost never refer to their family situation when they talk about their job and its advantages and drawbacks, and about their future. Single men also make no reference to the probable changes which would be introduced into their lives if they got married. Men, whether they are single, married or fathers, define themselves solely in terms of their occupation.

Women, on the other hand, even when they speak 'against the myth of the housewife', cannot define themselves only by their occupational status or their housewife status. They are always divided between an 'inside' and an 'outside', whatever their concrete situation may be. Single women do not escape this: their personal status, whether it is experienced as a free choice or as the result of chance, sought or accepted, only has meaning in relation to the situation of the majority of women. They are socially designated as lacking children, and, as such, 'incomplete' women. Some seek out this status thinking that 'work is more intelligent than baby-minding' and refusing to become 'cabbages' (in the words of the assistant to an advertising manager, who chose to live in free union with a man), but reference to a hypothetical or missing 'inside' is often implicit or explicit in the accounts of single women:

> 'It seems to me preferable that the mother should bring the children up herself, but personally I need an outside activity.' (Unmarried teacher.)

> 'Being unmarried and without problems, I can devote myself completely to my work. If I was married, this position would be too demanding.' (Buyer.)

> 'I like what I do, I hope only to progress . . . I was obliged to leave my family and my country to achieve this . . . I might get married. That would change a lot, especially if I had children.' (French teacher in Canada.)

The contradictions experienced and expressed by the women and the incoherences in their practices reinforce the incoherence of their 'me'. What are they? This devalued, closed 'me' or this free and powerful 'I' which can only assert itself in relation to that of the dominant, as its negative. In their own words ('I love Humanities', 'I've always dreamed of devoting myself to children') they are only reinforcing the splitting of their identity. This split can not be removed as long as the relations of dominance are maintained, as long as the dominated can only interpret their social condition by the logic of the natural order of things.

The dominated class

Through their class origin the children of both sexes in the dominated class have an equally dissociated identity. When analysing what the exercise of power by a fraction of the masculine population implies for the whole category of women, we saw the mark of the differences based on relations of dominance between classes. Like the women born into the dominated class, the men from this class know that their social origin has weighed on what they became. Whether they consider it to be a positive or negative element, it is a determining element in the unfolding of their existence:

> 'The influence of a master and the influence of a secondary college [CEG] . We only prepared for the *école normale d'instituteurs*, so we were subtly channelled, without knowing it.'

The constraints are imposed on dominated-class children far too long and in too imperious a fashion for them to think of their educational orientations in terms of pure freedom:

> 'The last teacher I had convinced my mother.'

> 'It was my teacher who put me in for the entrance examination in the *sixième*.'

> 'I was advised to go to the lycée.'

> 'It was the French teacher who found out that I was good at literature.'

> 'My teacher encouraged me by saying that I shouldn't stop there. He came home and persuaded my parents.'

> 'I took this channel because I lacked information and ambition.' (The son of a labourer.)

> 'My mother had been told that Section M was easier.'

Against the personal form used by the dominants — 'I chose', 'I decided' — is frequently set the impersonal form of the dominated (in English, the passive) — 'it was decided', 'I was allowed', 'I was permitted', 'I was given permission', 'they decided'. Also the 'I' of the dominated does not always have the same meaning as that of the dominant: the personal referent is object rather than subject.

Children of the dominated class are aware of having been designated as different, as marked with the sign of incompleteness:

> 'The people around me more or less knew that I was from a working-class family and hence I had a few hitches in that respect.'

> 'Some teachers used some very unkind words, saying that one was not society's rubbish, but almost.'

> 'I remember that the drawing teacher used to say . . . . He worked from the principle that workers' children couldn't understand art.'

> 'In hearing remarks to those with scholarships that they should make a greater effort than the others, because they were scholarship girls, I felt myself a bit vexed.'

It thus seems that they have a certain degree of insight into the social determinations that have weighed on their orientations. But this does not imply that they have a reflexive awareness of the relation between their class membership and their history. This concerns circumstances experienced as particular. They cannot escape the system of rationalizations which is culturally imposed. The daughter of an agricultural worker who was convinced that educational success is 'a question of money' added also: 'Personally I had ability.' If they have been distinguished, it is because they are particular. In addition, despite everything, they reinterpret their educational and occupational orientation by the dominant logic of taste and interest.

'I was interested in geography, in geography and history, as one may be in the *sixième* and *cinqième* and then later, given my educational background, there was nothing else I could do . . . it was fortunate since it interested me.' The same student further on: 'One thing I regret is not having done medicine. But I could never have been a doctor. It wasn't possible.'

'You see, I was tempted to be an archeologist because I adored ancient history, but for that you must go to the *Ecole des Chartes* and in the end, I really don't remember the train of events, but in addition you need a certain personal fortune to get there, and it's not really a woman's job . . . . So then I wanted to be a librarian . . . up to the time when I went in for teaching; but even so basically it was teaching since I was a child.' The same informant further on: 'I've always wanted to be a secondary-school teacher; when it's deeply fixed in you I don't think one can want anything else.'

'Teacher: it's a vocation. Now I like this job. I've learnt to like it.'

In these three cases, coherence was sought and reintroduced later on: 'It was fortunate', 'I went in for it', 'I've learnt to like it.' The dominant discourse provides them with the elements of singularization of the 'me' and with this they try to wrest themselves away from specification — the specification to which these women are doubly subject (as women and as dominated-class children).

What they are socially they consider to be due to personal and family qualities which distinguish them from their class:

'I'm going to boast, perhaps I was more successful.'

'My parents really took their responsibilities seriously; they are true parents.'

The implicit discourse is the following: We are workers but we are worthy, and we want to be recognized in the name of this worth. If there is an attempt to value themselves in the name of this merit, this dominant value, it is because they believe unconsciously (the unconscious draws its content from the dominant discourse) that to be a worker is to be dirty, immoral and shameful, it is to be 'less than nothing':

'I'm not ashamed of having parents like mine.'

'In my home there was a decent family life.'

'My parents managed to make a family life which was agreeable and everything . . . After all, many people remain less than nothing.'

'You understand, I can say that I was never ashamed of my parents. Indeed I admire them very much.'

All this effort and those of their parents are directed to the sole aim of proving that one is not 'lesser':

'I wanted to be the best because I'd been put down again.'

'I wanted to prove to myself that I was capable of higher education.'

But to want to prove to oneself and others that one is better than 'that' is to deny part of oneself and this denial engenders guilt:

'My parents sacrificed their lives for us.'

The comparison with others cannot be centred around a devalued and denied 'me', so it is polarized by the 'I' of the dominant which, for the dominated, is incarnated in the person they would like to be, in the first instance, a primary-school teacher (not a single dominant-class child said they had 'dreamed' of being a primary-school teacher), and then, a secondary-school teacher, an engineer, doctor, film director or higher civil servant. As has already been seen, the content of choices (teaching) often signifies the socially assigned limits to their desire 'to get out'. Even the most ambitious choices are marked by the experience of economic insecurity (a fundamental element of the class position of the dominated class) since stability of employment is taken into account. The ideal for one teacher was 'to be a higher civil servant of the *Ecole Nationale d'Administration* type – high for prestige and income; a civil servant for a secure job.' However, for men the gap between what they actually are and what they imagine themselves to be is smaller than for women. Also it is in women's replies that the dissociation sometimes appears in the form of statements:

'pilot, surgeon . . . or air hostess.'

'doctor or hairdresser.'

Dominant in imagination (who am I?), dominated in reality (what am

63

I?), the ego lacks cohesion, hence the contradiction and incoherence of the practices. Dominated-class children think in terms of aptitudes, tastes and interests because at each step in their education their success has progressively convinced them that they are not 'less than nothing' intellectually; but at the same time they profoundly doubt themselves. This doubt is certainly not unrelated to the split, discontinuous aspects of their orientations, as measured by the standard of a parsimonious and fleeting time. Their day-to-day projects, which lead them into dead ends or which build up gaps in knowledge which are inhibitory for their educational future, reinforce their doubts as to their capacities. They enrol at university:

'With the mental reservation that higher education could not be successful for the son of a craftsman or labourer.'

If they attribute their lack of success to the impossibility of doing both studies and a professional job, this lack of success weighs on the definition of their identity. Several years after entering the university they speak ironically about the pretentious persons, full of illusions, they used to be – persons whose behaviour now seems to them nothing but make-believe. If they enrolled in university it was:

'Out of snobbishness, to look good, for the pleasure of saying: I'm at university!'

'The puerile glory of being a real student at university.'

The relationship to his social being simultaneously lived and conceived by each agent is based on unconscious knowledge. What is designated as the 'subject' (the 'I') in the social discourse is the social being of the dominant. Thus in defining his identity the dominated cannot polarize the comparison between self/the others on his 'me' in the way that the dominant does. For him, according to the formulation of Frantz Fanon,[10] 'the directing fiction is not personal but social.' Just as Negroes, whose unconscious structure he analysed, saw themselves in dreams with pink cheeks, so the dominated whose class or sex are signs of natural incompleteness are unconsciously all-powerful; but actuality does not stop imposing itself on them for all that, hence the lack of cohesion in their practices. There cannot be a cohesion except on the side of power. Perhaps the dominated ignore that less than the dominant, as is clear through their accounts. Indeed, the more the practices of the speaker are the practices of power, the more the situation in which he places himself in the conceptual field is the mythical place where power disappears to the benefit of a purely abstract creativity. On the other hand, the more the speaker is subjected to power, the more he situates himself conceptually in reference to the very place where power is concretely exercised.

But by identifying with the dominant, by wishing to be defined as a pure individuality (in reference to the human being in general — the 'subject' — whose concrete support is the social being of dominants), they themselves specify the dominated with whom they refuse to be identified. We saw that the 'deserving' children of working-class families separate themselves from the 'less than nothing'; the independent women from the 'cabbages'. It is as if, in a social formation where power is unified, where acts of power exist as spoken acts, the 'ego' could not be structured without reference to an imaginary 'I' which is that of the all-powerful. But, while a unifying principle for the identity of the dominant (his actual 'me' — the set of his practices — and his imaginary 'I' being two homogeneous realities), the dominant ideology is a dissociating principle for the dominated (his/her imaginary 'I' and his/her social 'me' being two heterogeneous realities). The dominated are thus confronted with the impossible task of having to unify an identity which dominant discourse keeps dissociating.

A division or unity of the 'ego' could not be only interpreted in psychological terms: it is one of the constituting dimensions of dominance relationships. The facts of language have in this respect their own effectiveness, for language is not a mere 'reflection' of tangible reality. It is itself a social relationship. As we are going to see, dominant ideology acts as the principle ordering differential linguistic 'choices': here we are talking not only of the content of speech, its semantic aspects studied in this chapter, but also of its morpho-syntactic aspects. Thus, what remained obscure to most of the analysts who studied 'popular language' — linguistic 'differences' — may be clarified. As will be seen, it is as far as the imaginary referent (the 'subject', the 'I', according to which the 'me' is structured) is an element of dissocation of the 'ego' for some, an element of unification for others, that dominant and dominated cannot use identical linguistic forms. Each speaker uses lingustic forms according to the place he/she occupies in the structure of dominance relationships, according to the definition of identity socially imposed on him/her.

Notes

1 *Les Inégaux ou la sélection universitaire*, Paris, PUF, 1974. Here are a few details for those who are interested in the results of the empirical studies presented in this book:
   First study Who succeeds and who fails in the first year of university studies? A study on 6,919 students of *Lettres*, of the University of Paris, based on university questionnaires. Cf. pp. 74—99.
   Second study Who chooses which discipline? Who actually obtains a university diploma? The files of 3,345 students who followed

courses in *Lettres* were examined for four consecutive years. Cf. pp. 100–20.

Third study 3,242 questionnaires were sent eight years later to those who did not re-enrol after the first year. Who went on to study something else? What was the occupational and social outcome of social groups defined by their class origin and their sex? Cf. pp. 138–49 and tables pp. 188–202.

The facts observed cover the years 1962 to 1970. Since then, many transformations have taken place in the university system, but one can estimate as highly probable that the processes involved in orientation and selection are the same, just as inequalities according to class and age are the same today.

2 *Lettres* (which have become today *Lettres et Sciences Humaines*) included studies in literature, modern and ancient languages, history, geography, philosophy, psychology, anthropology, sociology and linguistics.

3 The percentages in this chapter refer to the tables on pp. 192–202 of *Les Inégaux* (see note 1).

4 *Collèges d'enseignement général* (CEG): four school years from sixth (*sixième*) to third (*troisième*) leading to the *brevet* (BEPC), whereas the lycées offered three years more (*seconde, première, terminale*) leading up to the *baccalauréat*.

5 The *écoles normales d'instituteurs* take charge of the fees and living expenses up to the *baccalauréat* of students who will be engaged by contract to teach in primary school.

6 The most prestigious higher education schools. There is a competitive exam at the entrance and they are in fact reserved to the 'well-born'.

7 The idea of women obtaining 'fulfilment' through work is held especially by those who have what they call 'free', 'independent', 'lucrative' jobs. It is sometimes accompanied by the idea that women should only work if they have a job 'they like'. Would this be the view of a class which defines work only as a free and creative activity? And yet some women, for whom work is all the more constraining as they are also in charge of family tasks, talk both of overwork and fulfilment; despite the psychological connotations of its formulation, the idea of fulfilment or 'freedom', which goes along with that of constraints, is full of sociological contradictions: work, which is a source of alienation for one class in general, can paradoxically become a first condition of release from alienation for the marginalized feminine part of this class.

8 Cf. E. Sullerot, *Histoire et sociologie du travail féminin*, Paris, Gonthier, 1968.

9 *Agrégation*: a competitive exam at the end of higher education which opens the best-paid teacher careers.

10 F. Fanon, *Peau noire, masques blancs,* Paris, Seuil, 1952.

3 Language and class identity. The mark of dominant ideology

Historically, dominant language and dominated language established themselves as such through relations of class antagonism. When one looks at the evolution of French language, one notices that present 'mistakes': *à cause que* (because *that*), formerly used to be elegant forms; conversely, certain expressions nowadays 'correct' are of popular origin: *soixante-dix* (seventy), *quatre-vingt-dix* (ninety) have replaced the previously prescribed forms *septante* and *nonante*. One notices also that the very notion of mistakes and the idea of having to correct them came into existence above all after verbal know-how had acquired a social value and had been controlled by a system of examinations instituted by the bourgeoisie when it came to power.

The forms imposed by grammarians from the sixteenth and seventeenth centuries were unconsciously chosen and codified by the bourgeoisie as being suitable to express and shape its identity as the rising class. This rising class became the social referent for the gradual reorganization of signifiers. Once the bourgeoisie had gained political power, through its practices (including its language practices), it constituted itself as the dominant class and the 'others' as the dominated one. It set up its own language habits (sign of its supposed natural superiority) as an absolute standard.

Specialists in the scientific enquiry on class languages have generally avoided questioning the significance of the dissimilarities observed between verbal practices. French linguists who, during the first half of the century, limited themselves to describing 'popular language' without making value judgments, gathered the data patiently and scrupulously. F. Brunot,[1] H. Bauché,[2] L. Sainéan,[3] G. Gougenheim[4] and H. Frei[5] are highly interesting, not only because their data are practically the only data available, but also because the forms listed are still in use today as showed by P. Guiraud.[6] However, despite the authors' desire for scientific neutrality, studies on 'popular language' are, in fact, no more than lists of exceptions to the norm. Nevertheless, comparisons between normative forms and 'popular' forms, between so-called correct and incorrect forms, add new elements to the definition of the identity of social classes. A new approach, then, allows one to go beyond formalistic analyses which treat dominant forms and 'popular' forms as if they existed *per se* independently of their relations, as will be seen in Chapter 4.

The hypothesis underlying our analysis of these relations is as follows: class languages are meaningful only in the light of the referent's social organization. Each class speaks itself, in other words, takes on and shapes its historical identity according to *the same hidden referent*, which determines the existence of dissimilarity in language practices today. This social referent is the class whose identity is based on what it possesses (including its knowledge and verbal know-how), the class which legitimizes its concrete power by defining itself as a collection of subjects, 'each free in his enunciative choices', as R. Robin[7] puts it. As will be seen, it is because the social referent is the same for all classes that it can produce a split between what can be called the language of power and the language of non-power.

The division of the reality into categories of beings classified under the same referent, man: something, someone, a person?

The delimitation of what is inanimate, animate and human
During the seventeenth century, the bourgeoisie, which laid down the law through its grammarians (especially Vaugelas), insisted that a distinction be made between words representing a person and those representing a non-person. From the sixteenth century on, due amongst other things to scientific practices, the 'subject', the observer, drew away from the 'object', the observed. A relatively more syncretic vision of the different modalities of beings, who had been given their place in the hierarchy by God, and were referred to God, a transcendental principle giving meaning to reality, gave way to a world view differentiating inanimate from animate and, within the animate, animals from humans, and finally dividing the latter group into different categories.

As man became the centre of reference for the defining and ordering of other categories, it seems as though the decline of the old world view, accompanied by a change of referent, rendered new linguistic forms necessary. Grammatically, people were differentiated from animals or objects; but under these circumstances the rules of grammar did not affect all social groups, so that changes concerning person nouns were not accepted as general usage.

In the seventeenth century, a complicated system of relative pronouns referring to people – à *qui* (to whom) as opposed to objects à *quoi* (to what) – was instituted, not without difficulty; one should no longer write, as Montaigne did: 'les Esséniens de *quoi* parle Pline' (the

Essenes of *what* Pliny speaks); and Vaugelas censured: 'C'est la table à *qui* je me suis blessé' (it is the table on *whom* I hurt myself). A further example of increasing differentiation in the perception of beings is shown in the suppression of *y*, which could formerly be used to represent persons; Vaugelas[8] writes:

> It is a very common fault among our courtiers to say 'J'ai remis les hardes de mon frère à un tel afin qu'il les *y* donne' [I gave my brother's clothes to so-and-so for him to give them to *it*] instead of saying 'afin qu'il les *lui* donne' [for him to give them to *him*].

Furthermore, a distinction was to be made between nouns referring to persons and common nouns: according to Maupas, and later Vaugelas, the former were no longer to be preceded by a definite or indefinite article – *le, la,* or *un, une* – as opposed to common nouns. Montaigne had been able to write: 'Entre les autres esclaves fut *un* Androdus . . .' (among the other slaves was *an* Androdus), but this form has become intolerable to Vaugelas: 'It is very bad and against the spirit of our language.' It was therefore laid down that to say '*la* Marie' (*the* Mary) was vulgar. Thus person nouns, called proper nouns, were accorded a special status in the hierarchy of words, and were not to be preceded by a determinant. Later, rules of grammar suppressed the use of the plural *s* for family names, thus breaking with tradition, according to which one wrote the Bourbon*s*, the Nero*s*.

Thus the use of an article preceding a proper noun became an exception: placing an article in front of a surname or Christian name was an attempt to give it the status of a common noun, to devalue the individual named. H. Frei considers that: 'When one says *le* Clemenceau, the *le* shows contempt.' Matignon[9] also: 'Formerly, one said *la* Champmeslé, *la* Béjart to designate actresses whatever their notoriety, then, by analogy, fashionable milliners and hairdressers, and finally all sorts of women whose reputation was not founded on virtue: *la* Brinvilliers or *la* Voisin.' Articles were therefore reserved for human beings who were denied the status of a moral person, or simply that of a person, in the sense given it in Lalande's *Vocabulaire critique et technique de la philosophie*:

> *Person* – Moral person: individual being in so far as he possesses the characteristics allowing him to participate in the intellectual and moral society of intelligent people [. . .] – Physical person: said of the body of a man in so far as this body is considered a 'phenomenon' of his moral person . . . .

As we have seen in Chapter 2, nowadays, dominant speech denies members of the dominated class, as also to other dominated categories ('race' or sex), the status of a moral person: the people are no longer immoral, they have become amoral; so according to psychoanalytical theory women are supposed to have a weak 'superego'. But under the Ancien Régime, certain acts were qualified as sins which could nevertheless be redeemed by divine grace, and all were sinners regardless of social rank. In the eighteenth century, once the old order had been overthrown, the new dominant class, the bourgeoisie, imputing the so-called vices and vulgarity of the people to the old forms of oppression, considered that everything could be reversed; everything would change in a society of free and equal citizens.

However, we know that as soon as the bourgeoisie had to protect its political power from the people, demanding equality *de facto*, it began to secrete an ideology based on the concrete relations it had established between possessors and dispossessed. So that its power would not appear to have been usurped, it had to substitute the nobility's declining principle of legitimacy with another. As it could no longer claim that its power derived from divine right, the bourgeoisie sanctified the elements in whose name it had seized power from the nobility (knowledge, merit, ability, etc.). It transformed them into intrinsic qualities which defined it alone, in order to legitimize its domination.

In the course of the nineteenth century, moreover, political practice enlisted the support of scientific practice, which looked for and found what had been assumed from the outset: power relations amongst groups of human beings are founded on a biological nature. Incapacity, improvidence, irresponsibility, amorality became inherent characteristics of the people and were supposed to explain its deplorable and, in fact, deplored 'condition'. Nisard,[10] who published a study of popular language in 1872, clearly assumed that the people must be 'lacking' something; in his view, the people's 'faulty', 'illogical' and 'degenerate' language was the direct consequence of deficient intelligence and natural incapacity: 'The people's thick tongue does not always manage to render easily the vibrancy of the high-pitched sound represented by the vowel *i*'; and elsewhere: 'All is contradiction in the people's language, as in its mind.' Other linguists who are attentive to the forms of dominated language have tried to break with essentialist ideology, but qualify as persons only the members of their own class, without being aware of the fact.[11]

In the present state of social relations, how can speakers of the dominated class comply with grammar rules on proper nouns? Can they name themselves or state their identity in the same way as those of the dominant class, whose concrete and linguistic practices reject them as unnamable? They invariably find themselves excluded from the definition of person, in the traditional humanist philosophy's sense of the word. Unable to define themselves socially as 'someone', dominated speakers are obliged either consciously to assert themselves incognito (Malcolm 'X'), or unconsciously to sink into the category of 'something'. This is the reason for the frequent use of the article preceding a proper noun, whether surname or Christian name, and expresses class unconscious knowledge: the identity of a fully fledged human being is socially denied to the dominated.

In the words of H. Frei, not only does 'popular speech explicitly determines Christian names: *"le* Charles est toujours dan la fournaise" (*the* Charles is still at the furnace)', but it also replaces proper nouns which singularize or personalize by so-called common nouns. Brunot states that: 'Nicknames are frequent in popular language. Sometimes they are added officially to the patronym, at times even replacing it. This is why they are often found in the records of the law courts and even in birth, marriage or death certificates.' To be sure, most of the dominant class's current surnames are former nicknames. According to Brunot, it is only in the eighteenth century that the surnames of people of modest descent became fixed definitively. The fact that these names assumed their definitive shape and spelling in the nineteenth century is not entirely dissociated from the simultaneous establishment of the bourgeoisie's social order: registers on which the name is stated were of paramount importance to a class which built its juridical system around the transmission of patrimony. As the social system imposed by the bourgeoisie refers one's identity to one's assets, surnames are obviously more important for the possessing class than for the non-possessing class.

Even metaphors are significant of the uncertainty of the dominated as to their identity. Most specialists on 'popular language' have been struck by the metaphoric use of animal names or allusions to animals to designate people or parts of the human body. According to Bauché: 'One often hears *cuir* (leather) or *couenne* (pigskin) for *peau* (skin), *lard* (lard) for *graisse* (fat), *vêler* (to calve) or *pondre* (to lay eggs) for *accoucher* (to give birth), etc., used with the obvious intention of comparing man with animals.' Of course, speakers of the dominant class also employ this kind of metaphor, but only when speaking of others. Speakers of the dominated class, on the contrary, apply these metaphors to themselves and occasionally even valorize them: the word *gueule* (snout), for example, is preferred to the word *visage* (face) or *bouche* (mouth); H. Frei gives this example: 'une bonne *gueule*' (a good looking 'mug').[12]

Less precise delimitation between the world of men and that of objects can be observed in other linguistic practices: 'Those whose names one does not remember are called *chose* (thing)', remarks L. Sainéan, who also notes the use of *machin* (whatsit), derived from the earlier *machine* (machine), to indicate anybody whose name has slipped one's memory. F. Brunot observes another significant fact:

71

'Instead of a word designating the inhabitants of a country, town, etc., the name of the town is sometimes preceded by the plural article: *les* Carpentras.' Conversely, some objects are referred to by proper nouns: Jules and Thomas signify a vase, Jacques or Jacqueline a cane, etc. Despite Vaugelas, *y* is still used for persons instead of designating only things or places: 'J'*y* ai parlé' (I spoke to *it*) and not 'je lui ai parlé' (I spoke to him).

Needless to say, these metaphoric usages invariably betray a distancing, and are not an expression of a syncretic vision of the animal, vegetable and mineral kingdoms. Nevertheless, they reveal that the dominated integrate the vision imposed by the dominant, which establishes different modalities of being amongst humans. Devalorized, rejected, defined as essentially 'others', those dominated are consequently more uncertain of their identity. Their uncertainty is expressed not only by the unconscious choice of metaphors, but also by the context in which they are used: 'On [n'] est pas des chiens' (we aren't dogs), 'on [n'] est pas des boeufs' (we aren't bulls). These suggestions deny what the dominant class asserts by its practices; none the less, this denial reveals a lack of certainty about one's own identity, if only because it tacitly assumes the primary assertion. The dominant group forces those whom it treats as objects also to define themselves as such, so that the status of subject is granted exclusively to the former. Even if the dominated refuse to accept this definition (we are not . . .), they cannot speak themselves as subjects like the dominant.

Differentiation within the human kind

The general relegation of the dominated to the sphere of non-person may explain their tendency to indicate less explicitly and less repetitively the difference between the male and female genders. In scholarly language at least, the inherent dissymmetry in the modern system of pronouns between *il* and *elle* (he, she), *ils* and *elles* (they m., they f.) established itself definitively at the end of the sixteenth century. Previously there had been, as G. Moignet[13] points out, 'several aborted attempts in the language to neutralize the opposition of the genders', during the era of Middle French. In dialects of the east and north, notes Moignet, *il*, the nominative pronoun in the singular, stands for individuals of the feminine just as easily as of the masculine sex. And most important of all, he observed a general, and no longer regional, phenomenon:

In Middle French, the use of *ils* as the third person feminine plural was so widespread as to justify the belief that there was a strong tendency to neutralise the opposition of genders in the nominative personal pronouns [. . .] . Marot's *Oeuvres*, Rémy Belleau's *Journal d'un bourgeois de Paris*, furnish many more examples of this.

From the sixteenth century on, when married women lost their legal rights and the social category of children was created, as P. Ariès noted in his admirable analysis,[14] the status of person was refused to the social group of women, thereby defining the identity of the group in power, the bourgeois, 'Men' in all the new senses which the word *then* assumed. The establishing of different hierarchic relations can be noticed in the rules which grammarians sought to impose. First, that *il* no longer be used indiscriminately; second, in the seventeenth century, that new rules also require even more marked forms, the grammar forms of the feminine, to be used in a redundant manner: rules on the agreement of past participles with the subject — *elle* est étonn*ée, il* est étonné (she is astonished, he is astonished). So that, while a new social differentiation was being established, it was expressed and reinforced by the dissymmetry in grammar forms.

This dissymmetry, which reflected the increase of hierarchy, was to become more and more marked when the bourgeoisie triumphed in the nineteenth century; *il* and *elle* related to categories defined as increasingly heterogeneous within the human kind: the 'good' gender and the 'bad' gender. Hence the significance nowadays of disparities in the organization of personal pronouns, which E. Ortigues[15] has analysed extremely well:

> In French, personalization occurs precociously as is shown by the dissymmetry of *il* and *elle*. Only the feminine subject pronoun *elle* is used also [. . .] as a prepositional complement: 'pour *elle*'; but one cannot say 'pour *il*' (for *he*) [. . .] . The word *il* is more rigorously subject to the mechanism of personalisation. This example is of great theoretical import: it demonstrates that categories such as 'object' or 'person' do not exist on a pure level in language, that is as pure concepts; they exist only through the significance given them by the opposition of existing forms . . . .

Having recalled the general (both masculine and feminine) use of the singular *il* and the plural *ils* forms during the era of Middle French, Moignet concludes: 'The language has preferred to adopt the somewhat hybrid system of feminine forms described above.' Is it really 'the language' . . . or the dominant class which imposed 'its' own language on its social order? In truth, how could this be 'required by the system', as the author repeats *ad infinitum*, since only a minority of French speakers actually expressed this difference in their language practices? The great majority always tended to generalize rather than individualize genders. Moignet, moreover, did not ignore the fact: 'This tendency remains widespread in popular language regardless of regional boundaries [. . .] . Even today, popular French tends to cancel the difference in the gender of personal pronouns, both in the singular and the plural.'

Not that other language forms in which the hierarchy of sex categories is indicated should be ignored. Where dominant language uses
personal pronouns (*ils, elles*), Bauché and Frei report the use in popular
language of a demonstrative pronoun *ça* (that or it), a term of indeter-
mination applied especially to collectivities. Now, according to the
examples given by these authors, it is not just a case of any collectivity,
but more precisely of categories of age and sex socially oppressed even
within the dominated class. Taken from Bauché: 'Les femmes, *ça* veut
toujours plus qu'on leur en donne' (women *it* always wants more
than one gives them); taken from Frei: '*Ça* joue, *ça* rit, *ça* s'amuse, *c*'est
gentil – en parlant d'enfants' (*it* plays, *it* laughs, *it* is fun, *it* is sweet –
talking of children).[16]

But the intent to devalue is also accompanied by the implicit knowledge that it is only a question of a degree more or less in the apersonal-
ization endured and experienced by all. The fact that the status of
person is denied to the social group 'women' does not confer this
status on those who oppress them as sexed beings within the midst of
the dominated class. Concretely and symbolically treated as objects,
regardless of their sexed group, men and women of the dominated class
differentiate masculine and feminine genders less obsessionally than
dominant language, maybe because the powers that be treat them all in
the same way. Indeed, 'correct' speech, with which the people do not
conform, imposes pleonastic usage of marked forms, which Frei points
out as unnecessary for the transmission of information: 'Distinguishing
the forms *elle* and *il* is superfluous where a noun of defined gender is
referred to by a pronoun.' Dominated language, which in other cases
abounds in superfluous usages, deals with categories of sex more homo-
geneously. This does not mean that genders are mixed up, but that
generalization is preferred to specification. 'The people [. . .] say *il* for
elle all the time' according to Nisard; and Frei gives the following
example: 'ma femme, *il* est venu' (my wife, *he* came).

Division of the real into categories of beings differs for dominant
and dominated. Distinctions appear less precisely among the dominated
who question their identity: what am I? Something, someone, a person?
They cannot conceive themselves as human beings outside the definition
of Man, the social referent, whose incarnation is the dominant group.

Singular being, 'subject' of the action/plural being, part of a process

The dominants' language practices are those of speakers who perceive
and express themselves as a collection of individuals, each defined as a
whole, as a collection of active wills, subjects of the action and of
history. In contrast, the dominated class's speech is more centred on a

process expressed by the verb, on the representation of an action taking place here and now, which is experienced as much as acted out by an anonymous and collective whole.

The 'subject' as social referent, and the grammatical subject

Once again, the study of the grammarians of the sixteenth and seventeenth centuries yields useful information of the usages of the period, which permits us to draw at least a parallel between changes in the objective relations of power and changes in language practices and their role in society.

The grammatical subject became articulated and assumed a preponderant position in the sentence once the bourgeoisie acquired a stronger grip on things and people, when, thanks to the system of selling office, it held the reins not only of commerce and manufacture but also of the finance and administration sectors.[17] In a society which changed to a monetary type of economy and consequently in which relations of dominance were being modified, concepts of language were also transformed. The idea of 'logical' analysis prevailed: compulsory word order within the phrase, where the subject must come first, became necessary in order to reflect a hierarchy amongst words as it existed between groups of humans. J.-C. Chevallier,[18] historian of syntax, clearly demonstrated how the bourgeoisie expressed and imposed their world vision by their manipulation of the language:

> To my mind [he writes in the conclusion of his thesis] the open
> pedagogy of the Renaissance, based on a mimetism of life, a life open
> to all, was replaced by closed, class-restricted education. Learning
> the language, an experience of immediate reality, became the affair
> of reasoned beings and reserved to the privileged. This favoured the
> elaboration of a syntax, structured wholly by 'reason', which included
> a theory of the 'complément'[19] revealing the logical relations which
> underlie a statement. The notion of 'complément' forms an integral
> part of the reasoning powers which the bourgeoisie forged for itself
> as an instrument of thought.

Thus the impersonal construction, which places the action to the fore and leaves the subject of the action in the background, lost importance during the sixteenth century and after. Little by little, in written texts, the verb gave way to the subject as the centre of a phrase, but it was really only in the seventeenth century that the use of the subject pronoun became compulsory. According to Malherbe, who still omitted the pseudo-subject *il* in impersonal expressions such as '[il] faut' ([one] must), '[il] semble' ([it] seems) and '[il] y a' ([there] is), personal pronouns which are the subject must always be expressed. Ronsard also advocated this rule. However, Rabelais and Montaigne frequently left out the subject, and there was still some hesitation until the seventeenth century, as Vaugelas himself held that this omission was sometimes 'very graceful'. However, a lover of 'beautiful language', he admitted that one should not abuse this omission. Some of his other remarks point toward the increasing importance of the subject; for example, Vaugelas was shocked by 'mistakes' in the agreement of verbs placed after a relative pronoun relating to a proper noun (the verb agreeing with a subject in the first person must no longer be in the third person).

Another rule reveals that the focus was shifting from the action in itself to the action's effects on the agent: such is the significance of the change from the form 'j'*ai* sorti' to 'je *suis* sorti' (I have gone out). Vaugelas writes: 'It is a common mistake to conjugate the preterites of these verbs "entrer" (to come in), "sortir" (to go out), etc. with the auxiliary *avoir* (to have) instead of *être* (to be).' In the seventeenth century, of course, one meets with innumerable phrases contradicting rules about the use of the auxiliaries *être* and *avoir*; nevertheless the process which changed the system of perception of reality had begun, and the act disappeared, giving way to the state, expressed by the perfect.

The grammatical subject, therefore, came into its own at the same time as man became the referent for the social discourse. It is not possible to talk of class consciousness as yet, in the classic sense of the word, reflexive consciousness; but that a new ideology was being born can be seen, among other social practices, in language practices. The idea of the individual as subject did not get under way until the eighteenth century, but the notion that history was made by active wills had already spread through the bourgeoisie at the same time as it had real possibilities to exercise power. Be it lineage in the case of the nobility or a village community in the case of the peasants, the vision of human beings entirely defined by their adherence to a community, part of a whole and having no social existence outside it, started to give way to the perception of separate individuals.

When the social referent changed, it would seem as though there arose a necessity to articulate the grammatical *je* (I) differently with other signifiers, thereby making it the point of focus. Indeed, a rule was laid down to this end: *je*, singular pronoun, must have a singular verbal ending, for example: *je* soup*e* (I dine), *nous* (we) soup*ons*, and no more *je* soup*ons*. Formerly, the use of a plural verbal ending with the first person singular pronoun was frequent, even among educated people: 'Among the courtiers, the best speakers say "j'all*ons*", "je ven*ons*", "je soup*ons*", etc.' observes H. Estienne,[20] who qualifies the usage of this form as plebeian. In the eighteenth century, F. de Callières[21] was still able to write: 'If, for example, a man of standing were to say "j'ét*ions* à Paris et j'en part*îmes* pour Versailles", he would be speaking like the common people' – a remark which presupposes widespread usage of this form outside the people.

During the seventeenth century too, usage of a collective possessive pronoun tended to disappear, which also denotes the same process of individualization. Brunot remarks that, in those days, women of the bourgeoisie living in towns used to say *our* neighbourhood, and not *my* neighbourhood, and he adds: 'This usage, which recalls the days of communities, has not completely disappeared yet in the language of religious orders. But, little by little, this use of the collective adjective was considered fit for the people and for servants, who used to say *"notre* maître" (our master).' Later, *je* was to be radically differentiated from *nous*. Even *nous* was to denote individuality of sorts by taking on a distributive significance; Ortigues considers that: '*Nous* individualises, singularises, and constitutes a complex moral person', and he further opposes this complex moral person *moi et toi* (me and you) to *je*, the single person. But for the dominated, *nous* does not have this significance and does not represent a set of subjects, all *je*.

The use of on (one) by 'those people'
Dominant speech certainly assigns each one his/her place, but only the dominant each have their place, the same one in all occurrences. For, they perceive themselves as a collection of singular beings, and apart from this collection of unique individuals in which they are included, they only distinguish masses of undifferentiated elements: 'the people', 'the black', 'women'. Indeed, in the world order created and articulated by the dominant, the dominated have no individuality or singularity, and particularities attributed to their group suffice to define them completely. The expression 'ces gens-là' (those people) indicates by *ces*, rejects by *là*, and expresses the idea of an undifferentiated whole. It comes as no surprise, then, that in the language of the rejected the word *ceux* (those) has lost its quality of demonstrative pronoun to become a noun. Brunot and Frei note following utterances: 'les *ceux* de Paris' (*those* of Paris), les '*ceuss* de d'par ici' (*those* who live around here).

Popular tendencies to pluralize rather than individualize are frequently reported by linguists. According to Brunot: '*Chaque* (every) and *chacun* (each) come to have a significance close to *tous* (all)'; and Bauché: '*Chacun*, rare in popular language, is translated by *tous les gens* (all the people).' Thus the concept of individuality is imprecise among the dominated. Rather, they seem to show a perception of a collective reality, composed of interdependent elements existing exclusively inside and through these relations of interdependence. In any case, the concurrent use of both the singular and the plural in an utterance proves that notions of individuality and plurality are not seen as mutually exclusive. The plural *tous* is sometimes followed by a verb in the singular, as in 'tous vien*t*' (they all come*s*) instead of 'tous vien*nent*'. Conversely, *tout le monde*, singular, often agrees with a plural verb. According to Brunot and Frei, examples of plural verbs following singular collective nouns abound: '*Le* manouvrier représente qu'*ils* ne peuv*ent* gagner . . .' (the skilled worker points out that *they* cannot earn . . .); '*Le* reste *sont* partis' (the rest *have* gone).

Another example of indifferentiation between singular and plural is to be found in the use of words representing people. It seems that speakers of the dominated class do not unconsciously establish themselves as the original and singular source of an utterance, but rather as a transmitting element of the group they are a part of. At the end of the nineteenth century, Nisard[22] was shocked by a locution which in those days was used in the popular language of Paris: '*j'nous* v'là' (*I we* [am] here). In his book, one sees that the personal pronoun for the first person plural can either be *nous*, the dominant form, or *je*, the form kept for the first person singular in normative language. Furthermore, as in the days when Vaugelas corrected the courtiers, the personal pronoun *je* is sometimes followed by a plural ending in the verb: 'j'all*ons*' instead of 'je vais' or 'nous allons' – 'je ven*ons*' instead of 'je viens' or 'nous venons'.

Apparently the plural form invades the singular form with its meaning, but the prevalence of plurality does not *per se* imply the notion of a collective 'subject'; rather, it suggests impersonality. *Nous* is sometimes used in agreement with the third person, and *ils* can agree with a verb in the first person. Nisard notes 'nous *ont*', 'ils *avons*' instead of 'nous avons', 'ils ont' (we have, they have). As it agrees with verbs in the third person, the *nous* of the dominated class does not represent a collection of *je*, and is moreover rarely used as the subject. Furthermore, when speakers of the dominated class use it as object, they often accompany the pronoun *nous* with *autres* as in the expression 'nous *autres*' (we *others*). Examples taken from Bauché: 'C'est-i pour nous *aut's* que vous disez ça?' (are you saying that for us *others*?); taken from Brunot: 'Nous *autres* femmes' (we *others* women). This word *autres* is very significant, as it shows that the dominated are only aware of themselves in terms of the dominant language's definition which they consequently impose on themselves: i.e. as belonging to an 'other' kind of humanity, since humanity's perfect incarnation is supposed to be the dominant.

Speakers of the dominated class prefer to substitute *nous* by *on*, and sometimes use them together.[23] Bauché observes that: 'Popular language employs "on est" and "on aime" [one is, one loves] more often than "nous sommes" and "nous aimons" [we are, we love]: "*Nous on* s'en fout" [*we one* does not give a damn]; "*on* est parti, ma soeur et moi" [*one* went, my sister and I].' Grammarians, however, state that the pronoun *on* depersonalizes – but is it always a case of depersonalization? Indeed, a speaker saying *on* can be depersonalized only if he uses 'I' and 'we' in a truly personal sense in other contexts. The dominated cannot reveal depersonalization since the notion of personality is not included in their social definition. Therefore, when they employ the pronoun *on* it cannot be a matter of euphemism, of 'reversing an indeterminate person to a determinate person', as Frei puts it: '*On* pensera à vous' (*one* will think of you) as a substitute for '*je* penserai à vous' (I'll think of you). G. Deleuze[24] also seems to ignore differential usages of *on* according to social class. Indeed, he ends his remarks on a comment made by M. Blanchot, the philosopher, on the expression 'on meurt' (one dies), by saying: 'This *on* is that of impersonal and pre-individual singularity, the *on* of pure happening, i.e. "il meurt" [it dies] just as "il pleut" [it rains]', and he concludes: 'How much this *on* differs from its everyday, banal usage.' There is doubtless a difference, but only for the dominant, since among the dominated everything is – in a banal, everyday way and not exceptionally – 'simultaneously collective and private, individualized and generalized'.

Action in the doing or the agent of action
The dominant's essentialist vision of life entails a concept of history in which its course is only influenced by will; according the subject of the verb the central position in a phrase is linked to this concept of history. Among the dominated, on the other hand, the subject of an action fades into the background leaving the process expressed by the verb to the fore.

Usage of the verb *faire* (to do), where dominant norms would have the verbs *avoir* (to have) or *être* (to be), reveals a different understanding of reality: '*Faire* une maladie' instead of '*avoir* une maladie' (to be ill), 'ça *fait* cher de vivre en Suisse' and not 'c'*est* cher . . .' (it is expensive to live in Switzerland). These examples were taken from Frei, who maintains that to substitute *faire* for *avoir* and *être* is to 'disguise an idea of inherence as one of relation'; maybe one should say that it is to express an idea of relation and not one of inherence.

Another significant fact: all the specialists on popular language have noted that the auxiliary *être* – prescribed instead of *avoir* – is rarely used with the verbs 'sortir' (to go out), 'venir' (to come), 'monter' (to go up), etc. Utterances such as 'j'*ai* monté' (I went up), 'j'*ai* tombé malade' and not 'je *suis* tombé . . .' (I fell ill) accord greater importance to the operation than to the situation, as Benveniste[25] puts it. Thus when Frei relates popular usage of the auxiliary *avoir* to the 'need for invariability', since most French verbs are conjugated with the auxiliary *avoir*, he fails to appreciate the possibility of an unconscious choice of forms, more adequate for the expression of reality as it is perceived.

Moreover, this is confirmed by the exception 'je *suis* été' where the dominant says 'j'*ai* été' (I have been). Indeed, usage of this form suggests that, if it is a matter of their being, of their identity, dominated speakers use a pleonasm, as though they needed to reaffirm their status as beings whose definition is problematic. The fact that popular language has not adopted usage of the auxiliary *être* with certain verbs, which Vaugelas had already recommended, shows that only the dominant have changed the focus to the present consequences of a past action for the subject, instead of leaving it on the action itself.

The elements for class definition in question seem to be not only self-definition in reference to the social subject, but also the way classes relate to time. Doubtless, the dominated perceive the course of individual and collective history rather as discontinuous than linear. At least, Bauché observes that: 'Popular language often confuses the future and conditional tenses in the form "je voudrai/s" ' (I shall/should like). But he immediately adds that it is more a question of the future than the conditional, for the idea of condition seems to be absent. Maybe the idea of a future conditioned by the past implies a minimum of control over events, the possibility of taking one's distance from here and now.

The dominated cannot project themselves into the past or the future with reference to power definitely lost or assuredly probable, that is to say which they could exercise tomorrow in concrete terms. Thus, as the future is never certain but always hypothetical, the future tense's function is to express uncertainty, whether it is the future perfect or the future simple: 'il *aura fait* de la galette' (he *will have made* dough). Forms expressing doubt, fear and desire relate the source of the uncertainty to a world foreign to the subject. But, it is in subjective terms, by referring to the psychological subject, that the dominant express doubt, fear and desire through the subjunctive, which is quite unknown to the dominated.

The dominated often leave out of their utterances the grammatical subject representing an action's agent. Brunot talks of confusion between the active and the passive; but one should talk of a spontaneous rather than of an arbitrary choice of the passive, if, as A. Meillet[26] says, 'the true role of the passive is to express a process where the agent is not considered.' The frequency with which impersonal forms are used is remarkable and has, indeed, been commented on by linguists: instead of 'j'ai soif' (I am thirsty), Frei notes '*Il* fait soif' (*it* is thirsty). Finally, phrases without a subject appear with great frequency. Sometimes it is no more than the suppression of the pseudo-subject *il*: '[il] faut croire' ([it] seems). Sometimes the subject is also omitted where the dominant never forget to stipulate it, for example when it refers to the speaker. Frei: '[je] voudrais bien de tes nouvelles' ([I] would love to hear from you), '[je] regrette, [je] n'ai plus' ([I] am sorry, [I] no longer have any).

Therefore, one may conclude that a speaker makes an unconscious choice of signifiers and of their syntactic organization, depending on his position in the social scale. The dominant's choice puts more emphasis on the subject as agent, whereas the dominated tend to picture history in the making.

'I', first person, directing the world, and 'I', non-person, directed

All linguists agree that so-called nominative personal pronouns formerly autonomous – 'je, soussigné' (I, the undersigned) – now form an integral part of the verb. They reckon that these words are simple elements of flexion, the same as flexional endings. However, everything points towards the fact that these personal pronouns do not have the same semantic value for speakers of different social classes. What does *I* refer to? 'To something very singular and exclusively linguistic', says Benveniste: '*I* refers to the act of individual speech in which it is enounced and it indicates the speaker.' Nevertheless, does the pronoun of the first person refer to something 'very singular' for all speakers? And does it not refer to any other field than an 'exclusively linguistic' one?

Forms of address: the non-personal form of the third person
It is generally known that personal pronouns are important in forms of address and politeness as symbols of the concrete power relations between social class, age, or sex categories. A. Dauzat's résumé[27] of these forms' history demonstrates the relativity of their usage and significance according to the relations between dominant and dominated groups:

In the Middle Ages, there was a controversy over *tu* [familiar 'you', second person singular] and *vous* ['you', polite form of *tu*, second person plural] but high society already often made use of *vous*. In the seventeenth century, at court, even equals addressed each other as *vous* and one did not say *tu* to one's children, although one still said it to the servants. Among the bourgeoisie, parents said *tu* to their children, as also the master to his servants. During the Revolution, *tu*, which had remained in use among the people, replaced the polite form *vous*, but only partially and more in theory than practice (indeed, there were contradictions, especially since the *tu* employed to inferiors, in their eyes kept its quality of haughty affectation, leading to controversy over the elaboration of military laws as to whether officers should address the common soldier as *tu*). Under the Empire and the Restoration, the *vous* was upgraded once again, but its usage was no longer the same: in the bourgeoisie, one no longer said *tu* to one's servants, but, on the other hand, one addressed one's children as *tu* and the latter said *tu* to their parents from the last third of the nineteenth century.

Finally, A. Dauzat concludes:

Since we have started to address our servants as *vous*, we no longer like them to use the same form for us. We ask them to speak to us in the third person . . ., a custom which has its root in the seventeenth century and which was suppressed by the Revolution.

Can one, then, admit like Benveniste that: '*Je* and *tu* – or *vous* – are inversible, and no such relation is possible between one of these two persons and *il* or *elle*'? Indeed, forms of address in the third person ('the only one in which objects are predicated') play a perfectly precise role. Not, as Benveniste supposes, that this form itself changes significance: sometimes 'a form of respect which turns a being into something far more than a person', and sometimes 'a form of insult which can nullify someone as a person', as he puts it.

In fact, in every case this usage is a process which nullifies the dominated, whether they play the role of speaker or hearer. Forms of address in the third person are always used explicitly to mark social distance, a distance which is both expressed and enacted through speech. When a servant uses the third person, he does it under constraint, for the form 'Monsieur veut-il?' (would the gentleman like?) is imposed on him by the dominant. The third person is there to negate the speaker's individuality and eliminate a *je* which would implicitly assert itself in the form of address 'voulez-vous?' (would you like?), the 'you' supposing an 'I'. On the other hand, when the dominant uses the third person to the dominant – 'qu'est-ce qu'*il* veut?' (what does *he* want? for, what do *you* want?) – it is to show the hearer that: there is nothing in common between he/you and me, to show that he/you does not have the status of person. Therefore, one can see that the use of the third person always nullifies a human being, as long as one does not content oneself with analysing an utterance only by referring the pronoun to the individuals present at the time of utterance, but includes the dominance relations and the social referent. Since the third person's function is to assign the dominated 'his/her' place on the social scale, usage of the grammatical 'I' poses problems for speakers of the dominated class.

The uncertain 'I' of an utterance
In Ortigues's opinion, *je* denotes 'the personal identity of a subjectivity needing to identify itself and be identified in discursive communication.'

But not everybody can be identified and live his identity as a person, as a subject. For this reason, the dominated often use, instead of the more simple *je*, a special form to state themselves as subject of an utterance: *'moi* je' (*me* I), where the accusative pronoun *moi* precedes the nominative pronoun *je*. Bauché remarks that: 'Popular language uses *moi je* more often.' In statements such as *'moi j'*aime ça' (*me I* like that) the so-called emphatic form in dominant speech is no more than an everyday statement, equivalent to the supposedly modest *je* of the dominant. When the nominative pronoun is uttered on its own, it usually suffers an ellipsis — *'j'*viens'. 'The pronoun *je* is never pronounced entirely, with the full *e* sound', says Bauché. If dominated speakers objectify themselves by using the form *moi je*, the process of objectification is even clearer when the speaker avoids the use of even the first person; *je* and *moi* are often substituted by nouns, which are neither proper nor common: 'C'est pour *bibi*' or 'pour *ma pomme*' (that's for 'number one').

The insistent *moi je* and the alteration of *je* to *j'*, as if the speaker were avoiding being the subject of his utterance, recall certain extremely revealing remarks made by L. Irigaray[28] on specific usage of personal pronouns:

A typical utterance for hysterics is: 'tu m'aimes?' (you love me?). They leave the hearer to take the utterance upon himself [. . .]. It is the 'yes' or 'no' of the (you) which actually underlies the message as such, and by so doing constitutes the hearer as the sole subject of the utterance.

It should be remembered that hysteria is a pathological behaviour peculiar to dominated categories of either class or sex. For his part, B. Bettelheim[29] remarks about one of his pupils:

While he never came out of his autism, he began after a while to use personal pronouns in reverse, as do most autistic children. He referred to himself as 'you' and to the adult he was speaking to as 'I'. [. . .] Such talking in reverse, or in opposites, is not easy for a small child to do and further demonstrates his capacity for logic. It is not easy to talk consistently in opposites, to do quite well in getting across what is wanted, and never once make the 'mistake' of using pronouns correctly.

Irigaray's and Bettelheim's observations lead one to the conclusion that an unconscious logic presides over the usage of personal pronouns: the unconscious reflects the historic-social reality where the social referent for 'I' is the power embodied in the dominant.

Thus the *je* uttered by the dominated is full of uncertainty about themselves; as soon as they say *je* they immediately steal towards the use of an impersonal form, which shows that they think of themselves in the third rather than in the first person, as is imposed by the dominant discourse. Indeed, it is noticeable that the grammatical *je* does not necessarily agree, as in dominant language, with other forms in the first person, so that the individuality of the *je* ventured at the start dissolves during the rest of the statement. Similarly, the relative pronoun does not entail the agreement of the verb in the first, but in the third person: a dominant-language form such as 'c'est moi qui suis' (it is I who am) becomes 'c'est *moi* qui *est*' (it is I who *is*). Or else the nominative relative pronoun in the first: 'je *va*' (I *goes*), 'j'y *est*' (I *is* there). Finally, there is we *whom* is). Sometimes, a verb in the third person agrees with a pronoun in the first: 'je *va*' (I *goes*), 'j'y *est*' (I *is* there). Finally, they are changes in the pronoun's person, the reflexive pronoun of the third person being substituted for that of the first person. It is therefore not only in the form of address that social classes define their identity, but also in the selective usage of so-called personal pronouns.

Dominant 'I' in the centre and dominated 'I' on the periphery

Only the dominant express themselves as subjects of their utterances and organize their phrases around their own self, which coincides with the 'I' of the social referent. In dominant speech all is organized in reference to the speaker's person. According to Benveniste, demonstratives, adverbs, adjectives and pronouns 'organize spatial and temporal relations around the "subject" as point of reference'. The dominated 'I' is subordinated to the dominant 'I' which orders. This is why, in dominated language, the world is not organized in reference to the speaker's 'I'. Contrary to the rules laid down by language legislators, sometimes the possessive pronoun is left out, and sometimes the possessive pronoun of the first person is replaced by that of the third. For example, Bauché gives this form of addressing of a woman speaking to her husband: 'Embrassez *sa* petite femme' (kiss *his* little wife) instead of 'embrasse ta petite femme' (kiss your little wife). He also adds: 'In a popular family, the child says "*la* maman" (*the* mother), "*la* grand'mère" (*the* grandmother), and not ma (my).'

It all seems as if, in an imaginary space, the dominated speaker occupied a peripheral position in relation to the centre, which would be the dominant. At any rate, the usage of certain adverbs hints at this. Bauché writes: 'In French, if one wants to speak with precision, one says *ici* (here) when the place is close by, and *là* (there) when it is far, or further than what is meant by *ici*.' However, he notes that *là* is used more often than *ici* in popular language; it can just as easily indicate a place close by. Similarly, *voici* (here is) is very rare in popular language. One nearly always says 'me *voilà*' (there I am) and not 'me voici' (here I am). This does not mean that the speaker thereby situates his environment at a distance from him; on the contrary, he situates himself far from a central place; he is 'there' and not 'here'. Indeed, Frei mentions a significant expression: 'The significance of *ici*, in popular language rendered by *là*, gives the figure of speech "être un peu *là*" (to be *there*), meaning solid, strong, someone to be reckoned with. As a result of essentialist ideology, which pushes members of the dominated class to the fringe by lending them a nature dissimilar to that of the dominant, all speakers of the dominated class speak from 'elsewhere' and not from 'here' like the dominant. This 'elsewhere' is the place of non-power.

Is the dominated class's language, then, a language which decentres the subject, something which may very easily be happening to dominant language at the moment? Indeed, some intellectuals of the dominant class try in their writings and analytical work to question the significance of 'I' in speech. When the dominant avoid using the pronoun 'I', or replace it by 'he', in their written work, they indicate a withdrawal, a critical intention, a distance from naïve speech, in which those saying 'I' consider themselves as the singular source of what they utter. These new language practices – whose advent and historical circumstances should be analysed – may suppose and infer certain changes in the language practices of the dominant class. Nevertheless, they do not annul the dissimilarities between language practices of the social classes, they do not annul the dominance relations between those who speak-while-looking-at-themselves-in-the-mirror and those who hold the mirror. Spontaneous figures of everyday speech used by authors of the 'nouveau roman' do not denote so-called deconstruction but preconstruction, as they do for anybody. Even if they substitute the pronoun 'he' for the pronoun 'I' in a literary text, they neither consider themselves, nor express themselves in the third person in everyday speech, and the nullifying 'he' reserved for the dominated is not applied to them socially.

Decentrality, attempts to take one's distance, to reveal the non-coincidence of the 'I' in speech and the social being, presupposes centrality, which is only true of the dominant. Only they are homogeneous to the social 'subject'; indeed, there is homogeneity between their concrete being and the imaginary referent, i.e. power, so that their forms of speech necessarily correspond to their practices, including the written practices on 'he/I'. But the dominated never can take their distances nor decentre themselves: the distance is within them, it is their 'ego' which is dissociated, fragmented, since dominant speech, in fact, forces the dominated to identify *individually* with the social referent.[30] The dominated's search for a unified 'ego' gives rise to a passionate interest in the facts of language, and especially in nouns relating to identity. But their search and attempts to 'deconstruct' language presuppose the presence of a certain number of objective conditions, at least some power. For the dominated, the search for the united 'ego' cannot result in an attempt to decentre oneself as it can for the dominant – an illusion which could end up in the inevitable discovery of a 'specificity' (blackness, femininity) echoing the dominant's essentialism, for the historical content to which the unconscious processes are applied is essentialized.

To conclude, we will insist on a fundamental point: the analysis, opposing so-called popular forms and dominant forms, shows that it is not possible to study the social classes' practices while omitting the dimension of significance conferred on them by dominance relations. Each social group expresses itself through forms which are remarkable for the coherence of their significance, and performs non-arbitrary unconscious choices from all the signifiers common to speakers of the same language. One cannot say that such a form is exclusive to the dominant, another to the dominated; rather, significant groups of oppositions are disclosed. Dominant practices and dominated practices form a system: the apersonal and plural forms of the one correspond to the personal and singular forms of the other, as was shown above for the sub-system of representatives of the person. A dominant discourse centred on a 'subject' could not exist without a dominated counterpart centred on the doing (and not the being) of a social 'object'.

Dominant and dominated languages are the inevitable result of the existing social system but also the scene of a power struggle. Pejorative words of popular origin which designate the act of talking: *dégoiser, bavasser, jacasser, barjaquer,* etc. ('to rattle on', 'to jabber', 'to spout off', 'to zak', etc.) allow one to suppose that words are suspected by the dominated. They unconsciously know that the dominant impose their own definition of the world order through the totality of their practices, including verbal practices, and thereby justify their power.[31]

Language practices denote and create relations of dominance through the fundamental process of identification, whose unconscious logic completely escapes both dominant and dominated. Perhaps the principles of identity and non-contradiction are not so obvious for the dominated who have to integrate an identity *de facto* and an imaginary identity which are absolutely antinomic. According to M. C. d'Unrug's analyses,[32] contradictions experienced by the dominated assume the shape of disjunctions in speech, which is why their speech appears incoherent and fragmentary. But can one talk of incoherence? Since analyses of class languages are still of a formal type, the meaning of oppositions between recorded forms has remained unclear. Consequently, formal coherence and discursive coherence have been confused. We have just seen that discursive coherence characterizes the practices of the dominated as well as those of the dominant.

But this fact escaped the notice of researchers who wished to make class languages a scientific object. In the 1960s, a critical movement denouncing the ideological aspect of dominant theory (aptitudes) proposed another explanatory theory: that linguistic and cultural 'differences' between the social classes would explain why some fail and others succeed. School decides that the language of children from the dominated class is faulty. But researchers who aim at explaining school inequalities through linguistic factors ignore that the dominance relations are at work within language practices themselves; their approach consists in subtracting from social reality an element, language, which is handled in itself. This is the case in the practice, if not the theory, of the authors concerned who do not ignore class antagonisms. Once more, their approach reveals a failure to recognize the processes along which class practices are constituted as 'different' practices within the same global system, according to the relationship on which they are based and hierarchized: a dominated and non-reciprocal relationship. Although they refuse to substantialize aptitudes for reasons of scientific objectivity, critical authors come to substantialize linguistic practices because their research methods are still marked by essentialist ideology.

Notes

1 F. Brunot, *Histoire de la langue française des origines à 1900*, vol. 10, première partie: La langue classique dans la tourmente. Contact avec la langue populaire et la langue rurale, Paris, A. Colin, 1906.

2 H. Bauché, *Le Langage populaire. Grammaire, syntaxe et dictionnaire du français tel qu'on le parle dans le peuple avec tous les termes d'argot usuels*, Paris, Payot, 1920.

3 L. Sainéan, *Le Langage parisien au 19ème siècle*, Paris, Boccard, 1920.

4 G. Gougenheim, *La Langue populaire dans le premier quart du 19ème siècle, d'après le petit dictionnaire du peuple de JCLP Desgranges (1821)*, Paris, Les Belles Lettres, 1929.

5 H. Frei, *La Grammaire des fautes*, Paris, Geneva, Leipzig, Slatkine, 1929.

6 P. Guiraud, *Le Français populaire*, Paris, PUF, 1965.

7 R. Robin, *Histoire et linguistique*, Paris, A. Colin, 1973.

8 C. Fabre de Vaugelas, *Remarques sur la langue française*, Paris, 1647.

9 P. Matignon, *Comment on parle en français*, Paris, Larousse, 1927.

10 C. Nisard, *Etude sur le langage populaire ou patois de Paris et sa banlieue*, Paris, A. Franck, 1872.

11 For example, Brunot uses 'popular *language*' (an expression referring to a *thing*) for the dominated, and 'cultivated *person*' for the dominant: 'Nowadays, in popular language, "ils" (they) evokes more or less mysterious anonymous beings [. . .]. Said by a culti-

vated person, "ils" refers to specific persons'; Bauché reveals his prejudice when using the impersonnal 'someone' for the dominated, reserving the word 'person' for the dominant: 'For example, if in elegant circles someone were to say "sa dame" [his woman], "vot' garçon" [you' boy] and so on [. . .]. If on the other hand a person naturally talking the language of society . . . .'

12 Consulted in a law case, F. Brunot stated in a letter dated 7 June 1913 that the expression 'Ta gueule!' ([shut] your mouth!) should be considered by the court as having the meaning it has in the accused's social environment.It means 'Assez!' (enough!), in *Vie et langage*, vol. 77, 1958.

13 G. Moignet, *Le Pronom personnel français, essai de psychosystématicité historique*, Paris, Librairie C. Klincksieck, 1965.

14 P. Ariès, *Centuries of Childhood: A Social History of Family Life*, New York, Random House, 1965 (first French edition 1960).

15 E. Ortigues, *Le Discours et le symbole*, Paris, Ed. Montaigne, 1962.

16 It should also be noted that terms of endearment, 'mon lapin' (my rabbit), 'mon chat' (my cat), etc., in which animal names are employed, are used above all for women and children.

17 Cf. the analysis of N. Elias on the struggle between the nobility and the bourgeoisie under Louis XIV, N. Elias, *Die Hofische Gesellschaft*, Hermann Luchterhand Verlag, Neuwied and Berlin, 1969.

18 J.-C. Chevallier, *Histoire de la syntaxe. Naissance de la notion de complément dans la grammaire française (1530–1750)*, Geneva, Droz, 1968.

19 Translator's note: the word 'complément' in French grammar corresponds to the concepts of complement, object and extensions of the subject or predicate, in English grammar.

20 H. Estienne, *La Précellence du langage français*, Paris, Patisson, 1579.

21 F. de Callières, *Du Bon et du mauvais usage dans les manières de s'exprimer. Des façons de parler bourgeoises et en quoy elles sont différentes de celles de la Cour*, Paris, Barbin, 1693.

22 C. Nisard, *Etude sur le langage populaire ou patois de Paris et sa banlieue*, Paris, A. Franck, 1872.

23 Translator's note: Although we have translated *on* by 'one', it must be remembered that the French *on*, contrary to the English 'one', is widespread in the language of the dominated class.

24 G. Deleuze, *La Logique du sens*, Paris, Ed. Minuit, 1969.

25 E. Benveniste, *Problèmes de linguistique générale*, Paris, Gallimard, 1966.

26 A. Meillet, 'Sur les caractères du verbe', in *Linguistique historique et linguistique générale*, Paris, Lib. Honoré Champion, 1965.

27 A. Dauzat, *La Défense de la langue française*, Paris, A. Colin, 1912.

28 L. Irigaray, 'Approches d'une grammaire d'énonciation de l'hystérique et de l'obsessionnel', *Langages*, vol. 5, 1967.

29 B. Bettelheim, *The Empty Fortress: Infantile Autism and the Birth of the Self*, New York, Free Press, 1967.

30 Otherwise dissociation of the 'ego' ends in autism, hysteria or schizophrenia, in which case the 'I' which does not exist, even on the level of imagination, is not uttered, as Irigaray and Bettelheim have demonstrated.

31 'Il nous cherche des phrases' (he tries to confuse us with fancy language) was André Chénier's ultimate sin in the eyes of the revolutionaries, his accusers, who subsequently guillotined him.

32 M. C. d'Unrug, *Analyse de contenu*, Paris, Ed. Universitaires, 1974.

4 From the theory of differences in aptitudes to the theory of differences in linguistic 'codes'

The structural changes, which occurred after the Second World War, coincided with ideological changes in the elements used to justify power relations. For in official speeches 'democratization' became a recognized and asserted value. One also witnesses a change in scientific interests and in theories relating to the differences of scholastic success according to social class. The explicative theory of differences in aptitudes was replaced, in the 1950s, by that of differences in motivation and then, in the 1960s, by theories of linguistic and cultural differences. This critical current assumed importance in the 1960s, when the rules governing the functioning of the educational system were revised. In fact, they had to be modified in view of the broader social recruitment resulting from structural changes in the economic system. The social conditions were then at hand for a small social group which benefited from this 'democratization' to challenge the traditional theory.

At any rate, there was a tendency to have a critical attitude to dominant ideology and the focus was placed on the importance of cultural and linguistic factors in scholastic success. B. Bernstein is one of the first researchers to have shown the existence and importance of linguistic factors in scholastic success, thereby demonstrating the limits of the theory of aptitudes. Indeed, this researcher's work marks an important step in the history of research.[1] My purpose here is to query Bernstein's theory. As will be seen, Bernstein ran into epistemological difficulties; since he operated as if the linguistic field was autonomous, his explicative system did not make a real break with the traditional explicative theory. Indeed, although he insists on the importance of power relations, he does not incorporate them in his theory or in his empiric work. However, by confronting some of Bernstein's results with those of 'popular language' linguists, we came to the conclusion that language practices are also the theatre and object of power relations. In Chapter 3, it was seen that language practices are a social relationship, and that dominance relationships are expressed in discourses which articulate and actualize them. This is a fundamental point ignored not only by Bernstein but by researchers who have criticized him, such as Labov.

Sometimes, it is the effort to distinguish facts of language from linguistic norms which fails, as the referent remains the language of the dominant class, so that the language practices of classes are stated as intrinsically unequal. Sometimes, research in a direction supposedly opposite to the first one ends by making it seem as though these practices were identical, as though they did not set one class against the other. In both cases, although the authors' objective is to study the split between social groups belonging to the same cultural universe (which although unified is nevertheless not homogeneous), their analysis of language practices stumbles on a faulty conceptualization of the social classes. By always leaving power relations out of the analysis of linguistic data themselves, by referring them to a sphere outside linguistics, they fail to recognize an important point: class languages established themselves and continue to do so through a *relationship*, and in a manner which is neither relative nor arbitrary; language practices are a fundamental part of class identity, in the definition of which the system of symbolic perception of social relationships has often been omitted.

From the assertion to the negation of a hierarchy between class languages

A theory of the 'differences', postulating class languages as intrinsically unequal
Basil Bernstein's approach is based on the necessity to break with the theory which, imputing working-class children's scholastic failure to an alleged intellectual deficency, bases itself on the prejudices of essentialist philosophy rather than on scientific analysis. He finds it important to compare linguistic forms spontaneously used by children with language practices required in school so as to show which cultural processes of differentiation play a role in scholastic selection:

> The power relationships created outside the school penetrate the organization, distribution and evaluation of knowledge through the social context of their transmission. The definition of educability is itself at any one time an attenuated consequence of these power relationships (p. 200).

> In one sentence, while the division of labour inevitably exerts an influence upon the contents of education, the class structure and its legitimizing ideology regulates the classification and framing of such contents (p. 241).

91

To put the hypothesis of a relation between class structure and forms of speech to the test, he has employed subtle experimental techniques since the 1960s. Little by little, he queried his first results and clarified his basic theoretical concepts (thus the distinction formal language/public language gave way to the opposition elaborated codes/ restricted codes).

Bernstein uses the concept 'linguistic code' and says he is not interested in language, but in speech. His starting point is the hypothesis that if the 'codes' used by the social classes are not the same, it is because the meaning systems they refer to are different: 'The concept code refers to the transmission of the deep meaning structure of a culture or sub-culture: the basic interpretative rules' (p. 198). According to Bernstein, on the one hand 'rural groups' and the 'lower working-class' use one code, the restricted code, and on the other, 'an elaborated code is associated with the middle-class and adjacent social strata', but, in certain circumstances, this class also makes use of the restricted code.

What are the characteristics of both these codes? Bernstein says that they oppose each other first of all through the more or less predictable nature of the linguistic elements a given speaker uses: both lexically and syntactically, the restricted code is to a great extent *predictable*, and the elaborated code to a smaller extent. Further, Bernstein contrasts codes in terms of the generality of the meaning they control: in the case of the elaborated code, meanings are *universalistic*, i.e. independent of the situation, for everything is explicit; in the case of the restricted code, meanings are *particularistic*, i.e. speech has a strong tendency to be implicit, to refer to a particular situation. Finally, both kinds of code differ through the *social conditions* in which they appear: the restricted code appears in situations where social relationships are close, communal, founded on collective roles; the elaborated code appears in situations where social relationships are based on individualized roles, where the 'I' is the referent, says Bernstein.

In the author's opinion, codes are essentially *social facts* and he warns against false interpretations of this notion: 'It is also important to point out that the codes refer to cultural *not* genetic controls upon the options speakers take up' (p. 146). Bernstein insists upon this point on several occasions, especially since his research work has been criticized as supporting the ideology of aptitudes, as though he, and not those who subvert his ideas, had talked of 'linguistic deprivation':

Language is a set of rules to which all speech codes must comply, but which speech codes are realized is a function of the culture acting through social relationships in specific contexts [...]. This is a sociological argument because the speech form is taken as a consequence of the form of the social relation or, put more generally, is a quality of a social structure (p. 173).

Our research shows just this: that the social classes differ in terms of the *contexts* which evoke certain linguistic realizations (p. 195).

How does the class system determine the social use of codes? Bernstein says that it is because it creates a certain number of constraints that *limit* the potential linguistic possibilities of the less favoured, thus impeding their *access* to the elaborated code, which constitutes one of the upper class's *privileges*:

Access to an elaborated code will depend not on psychological factors, but on access to specialized social positions within the social structure, by virtue of which a particular type of speech model is made available. Normally, but not inevitably, these positions will coincide with a stratum seeking, or already possessing, access to the major decision-making area of the social structure (p. 79).

One of the effects of the class system is to limit access to elaborated codes (p. 176).

Since 'schools are predicated upon elaborated code and its system of social relationships' (p. 186), the scholastic backwardness of working-class children is explained by cultural factors: 'The relative backwardness of lower working-class children may well be a form of culturally induced backwardness transmitted to the child through the implications of the linguistic process' (p. 136).

Comparison or compared evaluation?   However, despite his concern for scientific impartiality, Bernstein does not manage to avoid a normative attitude, for the conscious desire to subvert an issue considered as ideological is not enough actually to succeed. The criticisms, against which Bernstein defends himself by reasserting his sociological viewpoint, condemn his approach, which does not completely break with the dominant interpretative system. Indeed, the author seems to consider intelligence, intelligence quotient, as a reality in itself, as if the intelligence quotient, whose distribution hierarchically marks social groups if not individuals, did not depend — just as codes do — on 'the basic interpretative rules' of each social class.

It is easy to understand that in his first experiments Bernstein, placing himself on his opponents' ground, took the precaution of 'holding verbal and non-verbal I.Q. constant' (p. 82). What is more, his definition of intelligence may seem purely operational: 'These planning orientations are independent of intelligence as measured by two reliable group tests and word length' (p. 91). However, he uses expressions which are surprising for an opponent of essentialist ideology, as they imply the idea of a fundamental and irreversible difference between the social groups — 'innate ability', 'innate intelligence', 'degree of competence':

'Irrespective of their levels of innate intelligence' (p. 81); 'They may be different *performances* for every degree of competence' (p. 146): 'They [the codes] do not necessarily develop solely because of a speaker's innate ability' (p. 146). One can, therefore, understand that Bernstein's detractors were surprised by the use, in his early works, of expressions which were indeed conducive to promoting the all-too-well-established belief in the poor classes' 'linguistic deprivation': a working-class child 'is unable to generalize principles', and 'has difficulty with abstract concepts'.

Moreover, value judgments on speech tend to echo value judgments relating to the speakers. To be sure, the author afterwards stopped applying such judgments to the speakers, but he continued to use a normative terminology when talking about the codes. This was not done deliberately, for he alludes to the difficulties in attaining scientific impartiality: 'One of the difficulties of this approach is to avoid implicit value judgements about the relative worth of speech systems and the cultures which they symbolize' (p. 186). Nevertheless, he makes perfectly explicit judgments by according positive characteristics to the elaborated code: 'delicate', 'subtle', 'complex', etc., and negative characteristics to the restricted code: 'rigid', 'simple', 'limited', etc.

It would seem as though, not wanting to make any judgments, yet perceiving that his description was not impartial, Bernstein attempted to re-establish a just balance between his judgments: 'Elaborated codes give access to alternative realities, yet they carry the potential of alienation of feeling from thought, of self from other, of private belief *from role obligation*' (p. 186). He draws attention to the fact that in those codes a 'lot of nonsense' can be signalled. As for the restricted code, 'It should not be disvalued' (p. 136), says Bernstein. He then makes an effort to revalorize what socially is not valorized, and to speak well, too, of the restricted code. An impossible task, which, however, Bernstein feels he can carry out by changing the course of his analysis. It is no longer so much a question of the characteristics of the restricted code as of the psychological qualities attributed to the working classes: 'Their language is based on a warm and inclusive relationship.'[2] In fact, he amalgamates judgments on the speakers with judgments on the stylistic qualities of their speech: 'It is important to realize that a restricted code carries its own aesthetic. It will tend to develop a metaphoric range of considerable power, a simplicity and directness, a vitality and rhythm' (p. 136). In fact, instead of carrying out a comparative study, Bernstein proceeds to a compared evaluation.

Hierarchization: simplicity/complexity   Although he explicitly declares that the elaborated code is not in itself superior to the restricted code, Bernstein nevertheless continues to take the language in use in his class as referent: 'An elaborated code is the basic code by means of which our experience of persons and things is objectified and a different exploration of consciousness made possible' (p. 253). It is hard to understand to whom the plural possessive pronoun 'our' refers in the above statement. Since Bernstein believes that each class uses a code relating to its specific experience, why should the elaborated code be the 'basic' code for the objectification of working-class speakers' experience?

In fact, Bernstein's egalitarian ideals are the source of contradictions in his speech. He comes to the following conclusion (which logically stems from the fact that he thinks linguistic oppositions to be linked to concrete power relations) that a profound change in the social structure alone would be capable of abolishing the linguistic handicap hindering working-class children in their studies. Indeed, in the hypothesis of the abolition of social privileges, the elaborated code would undergo a radical transformation, since it exists in its present form only in so far as it transmits the values of the dominant class, and is a function of the exercise of power which governs its 'experience of people and of objects'. It is further to be supposed that, in this hypothesis, the educational system would use a code accessible to all. But such is not Bernstein's reasoning: when he envisages the modification of social organization as the solution for the handicap of working-class children, it is with the idea that they would have access to . . . the elaborated code; which implies, since the condition for access to the elaborated code is to become a dominant, a society made up solely of dominants, without any dominated (and not of equals using *one* radically different code).

Bernstein's contradictions stem from his belief that the type of speech used by the dominant class represents a tool more perfected, more apt to facilitate intellectual development. He holds that children 'deprived' of the elaborated code are limited in their thinking and that their capacity to generalize and to conceptualize is hindered from developing fully. In fact, they 'lack' the linguistic tools (conjunctions, lexical forms, etc.) which would enable them to make abstractions from concrete situations, to transfer their speech from the realm of implicit-ness to that of explicitness: 'The net effect of the constraint of a restricted code will be to depress potential linguistic ability, will inhibit generalizing ability at the higher ranges' (p. 81); 'This code orients its speakers to a less complex conceptual hierarchy and so to a lower order of causality' (p. 151).

Bernstein's belief in the superiority of explicitness, which led him to the elaboration of complexity indices based on a sum of formal operators, reveals confusion of formal coherence with discursive coher-ence. A formalized, explicit speech is considered as a sign of more abstract, more logical and more rational thought. Although the rhetoric of scientific language here uses more sophisticated ploys than the

95

rhetoric of the discourse on aptitudes, the mathematical evidence nevertheless still plays the same role of obscuring the issue; the quotient of 'complexity' is substituted for intelligence quotient, but it still carries out the same ideological function. The outlining and analysis of the facts are still inspired by the idea that there exists a 'more' on one side and a 'less' on the other, for the implicit referent, in effect, remains the social 'subject', namely, the dominant group.

Reification of the codes and evolutionist view   While refusing to reify intelligence, Bernstein manages to reify language practices. Of course, he insists on the fact that his principal preoccupation remains the explanation of the use of different codes in reference to situations. He applied himself to explain the first correlations between class membership and the type of code used by undertaking, he says, the analysis of four types of situations with which families of different social classes find themselves confronted: 'the regulative contexts (moral order)', 'the instructional contexts', 'the imaginative or innovative contexts', 'the interpersonal contexts' (p. 198). This brought him to distinguish types of families within each class characterized by a 'particular orientation': families of the 'positional' type oriented towards status, this first type generally characterizing working-class families; and families of the 'personal' type, that is, centred on the person: 'By about 1962, the crude correlation between forms of language use and social class had been more sensitive, so that the basic unit had become a family type with a particular communication structure and focus' (p. 244). He then opposes two forms of elaborated code to the restricted code: speech centred on objects (for example, the language of the exact sciences), or on people (for example, the language of the social sciences). But the study of these mediations leaves the problem of the emergence and subsistence of class dialects unsolved, for Bernstein's later studies refined but did not invalidate the statistic regularities established in his first experiments.

In fact, an analysis of the processes whereby meaning systems and codes specific to each social class are transmitted within a family was carried out with the basic assumption that these codes constitute self-existing realities: such and such life experiences correspond to this meaning system, this value system, and this type of code. Bernstein defines and fixes the attributes of each code, but fails to recognize that the said attributes exist only in a system of relationships, that the codes are not realities which can be conceived independently of each other.

Bernstein's unconscious postulate is that of a transcendent reality, 'the' language, whose resources would be used to the fullest extent only by one class, the class in power; this class would prevent the others from having access to the perfected tool, whose use it would keep for itself. Although Bernstein thinks the codes as resulting from social conditions which tend to privilege different meaning systems, he declares: 'Elaborated codes are less tied to a given or local structure'; 'In the case of elaborated codes, the speech may be freed from its evoking social structure and it can take on an autonomy' (p. 176).

Moreover Bernstein's vision is evolutionist. Some of his arguments on the conditions of appearance of the different codes reveal his failure to appreciate the historical processes according to which a dominant and a dominated language were gradually formed. His interpretation of the present social reality seems to be the following: the elaborated code, the language of his own class, is the result of slow evolution, of continual progress towards a superior state. He makes it seem as though one class has remained at the stage of restricted code whereas the other was inventing a more perfect language, a language more adapted to the tasks to be accomplished, to the problems to be solved by man so as to dominate nature and constitute a corpus of scientific knowledge.

Bernstein refers to Durkheim: 'The concepts of restricted and elaborated codes took their starting point from Durkheim's two forms of solidarity' (p. 239). Now, according to Durkheim, mechanic solidarity characterizes pre-industrial societies and organic solidarity characterizes industrial societies (for in the latter the division and complexity of the tasks evoked, in his mind, the functioning of the human body's different organs). Bernstein's utilization of the concepts of mechanic and organic solidarity will be discussed further on. For the moment, let us content ourselves with underlining the fact that Bernstein sees the origins of the elaborated code in the increasing complexity of occupational roles due to the division of labour:

> One major source of the movement from restricted to elaborated codes lies in increases in the complexity of *division of labour.* This changes both the nature of occupational roles and their linguistic bases (p. 150).

> The first major source of change I suggest is to be located in the *division of labour.* As the division of labour changes from simple to complex then this changes the social and knowledge characteristics of occupational roles (p. 186).

Afterwards, changes affecting industrial societies were to create differentiated forms of the elaborated code: 'The two modes of the elaborated code may well be affected by the movement of economies from goods to service types' (p. 150).

The idea of social relations of dominance influencing the formation of the codes is notably absent in Bernstein's work. In short, a purely technical division of labour is supposed to have presided over the slow genesis of the elaborated codes in industrial societies. This is an evolutionistic vision astonishing in an author who is none the less aware of the importance of power relations in a class society and whose approach, he claims, is influenced by Marx's analyses: 'The major starting points are Durkheim and Marx' (p. 171).

The counter-current. Assertion of equality leads to a theoretical dead-end
Researchers who reproach Bernstein for having a formalistic approach found a spokesman in W. Labov, who objects to the construction of complexity indices.[3] But seeking to prove that class languages have the 'same' value, the counter-current, for this very reason, cannot bring about the necessary epistemological break, as will be seen.

The assertion of equality Above all, Bernstein has been criticized for restricting his analysis to the formal aspects of speech, to explicitness. To come to conclusions in terms of the degree of syntactic complexity by basing oneself on formal and superficial criteria means, says Labov, that one forgets the implicit aspects of speech. According to Labov, Bernstein let himself be deluded by the type of results depending on particular experimental conditions. One only has to vary these conditions to see that there is no univocal meaning in linguistic forms, that the same forms do not necessarily relate to the same signified, and that it is consequently aberrant to add forms like 'because' and 'although'. Bernstein's critics therefore insist on the necessity to reintroduce the mediation of meaning into speech analysis, which can be done only by knowing the elements of the situation, of what lies outside the linguistic field. By doing this, one notes that seemingly ambiguous, incoherent or fragmentary utterances are rarely so for those physically present.

Formalization is not necessarily essential, and the ideas of causality and consequence do not need to be rendered explicit by a conjunction so as to be transmitted and received. Bernstein confuses formalization and conceptualization because he keeps to the explicit aspects of speech and to an internal analysis of the linguistic data. The language penalized by the school system is neither less rich nor less complex, but simply less formalized. Trying to go beyond a type of analysis based solely on signifiers, the new current therefore insists that the elements making up a situation must be taken into account: when the situation changes, one can observe that the verbal behaviour of the children examined changes radically, so that the material gathered in a constraining school situation, where adults impose their questions, is quite relative. When a child is in front of an adult (teacher or psychologist), his speech varies in accordance with his perception and categorization of that adult: laconic, almost dumb when in front of a 'judge', a working-class child is capable of expressing himself in 'complex' forms, as long as the interviewer seems socially close to him and broaches topics of conversation which are a part of the child's universe.

Although it exists, the disagreement between Bernstein and the Labovian current is nevertheless not fundamental. Indeed, Bernstein has protested against the reductiveness of Labov's criticisms: 'It is a travesty to relate the concepts of elaborated or restricted codes to superficial stylistics of middle-class and working-class forms of conversational behaviour, as implied by Labov' (p. 242). He emphasizes that in his opinion the differences between the codes have always been related to the differences between the situations experienced:

> The basic thesis has been that forms of communcation may be distinguished in terms of what is rendered implicit and what is rendered explicit (p. 242).

> The second formulation in terms of restricted and elaborated codes represented an attempt to formulate the regulative principles which I considered to underlie implicit and explicit forms of communication (p. 243).

> We could also (with Professor Halliday's network theory) show the *different* linguistic realizations of different context *and* decide whether each context had evoked either a restricted or an elaborated variant (p. 248).

Labov reproaches Bernstein with restoring a hierarchy in complexity no longer between forms of intelligence, but between types of codes. Indeed, it has been seen that Bernstein has constantly sought to take his distances from dominant ideology but that he has failed in this undertaking as he only knows this ideology's conscious form, its most immediately accessible form.

In short, both Bernstein and Labov want to lay the foundations of an approach which breaks completely with that of the 'differences': but, whereas the former, as has been seen, still talks in terms of a hierarchic continuum, the latter as yet simply denies the existence of a hierarchy. Labov in answer to Bernstein: you say that the language of the upper classes is *more* complex than that of the working classes, but I shall show you that both languages are *equally* complex. Doubtless a necessary moment in the process of historic development of research on class languages, this phase of negation has accomplished no more than to take up these problems in the same terms as did their predecessors.

Just like the assertion of hierarchy, its denial also leads for the moment to a dead-end, for in both cases one central question is left out: how and why did class-marked types of speech come into existence? It is not enough to say that there is no hierarchy between languages, but in a research which gives the social determinants of the speech as its subject, the following sociological fact should be included in the analysis: only one code is valorized by all the classes as a tool whose efficaciousness in maintaining the social hierarchy cannot be denied. Supposing, then, that language practices (at least in so-called familiar language) are identical amongst dominant and dominated, this does not invalidate the fact that only the dominant class disposes of the 'elaborated' code. The refusal to valorize this code does not change the fact that it induces a split between speakers-of-the-same-language. At any rate, those who are 'deprived' of the 'right' language are aware of the fact that dominant language is an instrument of ideological domination.

The illusion of the evidence of a meaning: the 'implicit', the 'situation'
It is possible to criticize the current which refers the meaning of linguistic oppositions to a field outside linguistics for failing to recognize the fact that dominance relationships constitute class dialects including their morpho-syntactic aspects. If one can but agree with the necessity of reintroducing implicitness in speech analysis, one should nevertheless be on one's guard against the notion of 'situation' which can also muddle the issue. Indeed, it appears that the illusion of evidence denounced by Labov, when referring to studies which only take explicitness into account, remains a misleading element also where the extra-linguistic field is concerned. While linguistic analysis has become subtle the analysis of the elements of the 'situation', on the contrary, is still but a rough outline. This makes the so-called situation a nebulous notion, which reminds one of the equally nebulous term 'environment'. In a communication situation, are there concrete elements, whose meaning would be transparent, and could linguists introduce them as such into the analysis? Moreover, to vary the situation for experimental purposes so as to see what becomes of verbal behaviours is, of course, full of interest, but does it not create an artificial situation? For example, do speakers of the poorer classes often deal with 'questioners' (interviewers, representatives of various administrative offices, bosses, etc.) overflowing with sympathy?

A point of utmost importance is omitted in so far as there is complete silence about verbal exchanges between speakers of different classes. Bernstein's interest is drawn only to the process of communication within each class, but what of the exchanges between dominant and dominated? It is to be supposed that speakers of the dominated class who only dispose of the restricted code address the representatives of the dominant class in the restricted code. But how does the dominant class, which itself disposes of both the restricted and the elaborated code, behave? In which 'situations' does it use the one or the other code? In this class (as in the other), says Bernstein, the restricted code is employed for exchanges between people on an intimate footing, who share the same values and, on the whole, the same implicits: 'Communication goes forward against a backcloth of closely shared identifications and affective empathy which removes the need to elaborate verbal meanings and logical continuity in the organization of speech' (p. 147). In situations where speech does not need to be explicit or formalized, for example between friends or a couple married for a long time, the dominant class also uses the restricted code. In the upper classes, then, the code of intimacy, the restricted code, would, according to Bernstein, be unfit for exchanges with 'inferiors'. However, are comminatory orders given in the elaborated code? And if the class which gives them in these cases uses the restricted code, then surely this code is not necessarily that of 'affective empathy'? As for Labov, he chooses protagonists whose positions in the social hierarchy are not the same, so as to demonstrate the variations of form and content in speech, but he is not in fact any more interested than Bernstein in what is articulated *socially* when members of different classes are in each other's presence.

Taking this kind of 'situation' into consideration could have helped the authors to clarify the said concept. Whatever the case may be, it is hard to imagine that centring the description on concrete scenes necessarily leads to paying attention to the basic point. Whatever the situation, whoever the speakers present may be, dominated and dominant use linguistic forms adequate for the definition of their social identity. It is the social relationships of dominance which, expressed in speech, oppose linguistic forms to each other, oppose the 'codes' which each class disposes of. In the same way as it is necessary to probe beyond the empiric aspect of social reality to get at its structure, so too one should break through the stage of describing utterance situations to perceive that dominant and dominated forms can be analysed only through their relationships. Basically, there exists one single situation, the established universe of dominance relations, in which experimental variations are only so many infinitesimal modulations.

There is no need for the speakers to be involved in a hierarchic relationship for the reference to power, whether exercised or endured to influence the form of their speech without their knowing it. On page 82, it was seen that the meaning of personal pronouns is far from being complete when only the concrete elements of a situation are considered. In the expressions – 'Monsieur veut-il?' (Would the gentleman like?) addressed to a dominant and 'Qu'est-ce qu'*il* veut? (what does *he* want?) addressed to a dominated – one can see that the meaning of *il* (he) is in both cases an annihilation of the dominated, provided one does not stop at a linguistic analysis saying that in the first expression the referent is the dominant and in the second utterance the dominated. For in every situation, one and the same referent gives significance to the utterances: this referent is the group exercising both concrete and symbolic power. But it is a hidden referent, and is not immediately perceptible as a concrete element of the situation. It is in relation to this hidden referent that, in the social discourse, dominated groups and their members are particularized, categorized and globalized, as C. Guillaumin demonstrated so well in her analysis of the daily press.[4] When newspapers talk of a 'black' athlete but never of a 'white' one, when one reads that '4 terrorists have been arrested: 2 of them are women' but never that '4 terrorists have been arrested: 2 of them are men', can one say that the meaning of the utterances is exhausted by an awareness of the elements in the utterance situation? The meaning of differences between two produced utterances ('an athlete'/'a black athlete') or between the produced utterance (2 of them are women) and an utterance not produced but which is grammatically and logically possible (2 of them are men) is given by the discourse's hidden referent.

Bernstein and those who criticized him therefore ran into the same difficulty and ended up, although by different paths, at the same dead-end (since none of them account for the existence of class 'dialects' in the same cultural universe). In fact, they do not make a sociological analysis because they have no precise definition of the social classes. If they get round to reify languages (Bernstein turns them into hierarchized objects, Labov into juxtaposed objects) it is only in so far as they reify the social classes themselves.

Oppositions between class languages are given meaning by the same referent: power

'Social classes' and 'power relationships' transmuted into abstract objects

In the approaches which have just been mentioned, while the analysis of linguistic data has been thoroughly developed, one of the essential points of the problems raised, the definition of social classes, has been neglected. Occupation is the empiric criterion for the definition of class membership. But Bernstein employs the concept of class without integrating it into a coherent theoretical system. At times, the word 'class' is synonymous with stratum or social status in the sense given to it by American sociology: 'Class is only one of many principles of social stratification' (p. 81); 'Class relation, that is a result of its common occupational function and social status' (p. 143). Sometimes classes are treated as objects in themselves, defined by specific attributes: 'Certain demographic attributes of families, such as level of education and economic functions' (p. 244). Although Bernstein claims he borrowed the elements of his theory from Durkheim, Marx and Mead, he only adds phenomenological notations:

> The class structure influences work and educational roles and brings families into a special relationship with each other and deeply penetrates the structure of life experiences within the family. The class system has deeply marked the distribution of knowledge within society. It has given differential access to the sense that the world is permeable. It has sealed off communities on a scale of invidious worth. We have three components, knowledge, possibility and invidious insulation. It would be a little naïve to believe that differences in knowledge, differences in the sense of the possible, combined with invidious insulation, rooted in differential *material* wellbeing, would not affect the forms of control and innovation in the socializing procedures of different classes (p. 175).

These are disparate remarks which cannot be taken as a theoretical definition.

The classes are juxtaposed objects or lost objects   Durkheim's sociological ideas are subjected to a completely personal reinterpretation by Bernstein: 'The type of social solidarity realized through a restricted code points towards mechanical solidarity, whereas the type of solidarity realized through elaborated codes points towards organic solidarity' (p. 147) – an original comment which nevertheless alters the thought of the author of *On the Division of Labour in Society*. Whereas Durkheim contrasts mechanical solidarity, specific to a type of organization of work to be found in 'primitive' societies, with a new form of solidarity born of the diversity and complexity of the tasks in an industrial type of society, Bernstein applies the distinction to one and the same type of society. For, to attribute mechanical solidarity to the dominated class and organic solidarity to the dominant class is to consider classes as closed systems with a relationship of co-existence and not of reciprocal dependency.[5]

The method of approach is marked by this. Bernstein separates and dichotomizes so as to compare, as if it were a question of comparing, like an ethnologist, heterogeneous cultural systems and not two subsystems which define each other. In fact, when he talks of social structure, the expression 'social structure' does not refer to the whole society, but to each particular class, which, according to him, has 'its' social structure and 'its' social organization: 'These two codes, elaborated and restricted, are generated by a particular form of social relation. Indeed they are likely to be a realization of different social structures' (p. 146). Thus each class, a closed society, would generate *on its own* a system of valorized meanings: 'It is reasonable to argue that the genes of social class may well be carried less through a genetic

103

code but far more through a communication code that social class itself promotes' (p. 143). Social classes are thought of as entities and not as realities defined solely by mutual dependence relations.

One is tempted to ask what meaning Bernstein gives to the expression 'power relations'. One thing is sure: he does not reason in terms of class antagonisms. In his mind, the dominant class does not seem to derive its class position from the existence of the others; it represents a superior degree attained in the course of the evolution of the human species, and each human group is called upon to achieve the same level. As the elaborated code supposedly expresses 'the complex differentiated aims of the major society', and not the aims of the dominant class, each one should have access to it.

In short, Bernstein considers the identity of the others as potential since he imagines they are called upon to acquire the identity of the dominant. Indeed, it has been seen that in the hypothesis of a change in the social structure, he can envisage nothing but an egalitarian distribution of the elaborated code and of the meanings it expresses; he cannot imagine the existence of one or several radically different systems of meanings. Of course, this is a generous wish, everybody must profit 'from it', but this generosity betrays class blindness: he cannot imagine a better incarnation of human nature than the human beings of his own class; he remains convinced of the intrinsic superiority of his class's language.

Although he often alludes to power relations, Bernstein (and also Labov) thinks of his society as a diversified, stratified reality without class conflicts. Social inequalities are but hitches in the present social system and are about to disappear: he considers that in view of the improvement of living standards, of rehousing policies, etc., the conditions for the working class to accede to the elaborated code are at hand: . . . there now exist the *conditions* for more individualized and less communalized relationships' (p. 162). In truth, Bernstein confuses equality *de facto* with an egalitarian system of values:

> The second major source of code orientation is likely to be the character of the central value system. Pluralistic societies are likely to produce strong orientations towards the person mode of an elaborated code, whereas monolithic societies are likely to strengthen the orientation towards the object mode. It should be remembered that persons can be treated as objects (p. 150).

Does this mean that in pluralistic societies (such as the USA and UK, p. 173) all human beings would no longer be treated as objects but as 'subjects'?

Psychologism and voluntarism   For Bernstein, the expression 'social structure' is equivalent to interpersonal relations, so that, contrary to what he thinks, his thesis is not sociological but derives from reductionist psychologism. There is never any question of *social relations* but of *intersubjective relations*:

> Changes in the form of certain social relations, it is argued, act selectively upon the principles controlling the selection of both syntactic and lexical options [. . .] . The speech used by members of an army combat unit on manoeuvres will be somewhat different from the same members' speech at a padre's evening [. . .] . This is a sociological argument, because the speech system is taken as a consequence of the form of the social relation or, to put it more generally, is a quality of the social structure (p. 124).

There is no question of *social relations of production* but of '*roles*'. The notion of 'role' is not only central but causal in Bernstein's theory:

> We have now outlined a framework which shows a causal connection between role systems, linguistic codes and the realization of different orders of meaning and relevance. Emphasis has been laid upon the relationship between roles and codes (p. 149).

> Different role options were made available in these hypothetical types of families and I connected causally the nature of these role options with the nature of the linguistic options (p. 244).

However, Bernstein's definition of his concept of role is vague:

> A role is a constellation of shared learned meanings, through which an individual is able to enter into persistent, consistent and recognized forms of interaction with others (p. 125).

> Role is defined as a complex coding activity controlling the creation and organization of specific meanings and the conditions of their transmission and reception (p. 171).

Why do workers' children use the restricted code and middle-class children the elaborated code? Because, Bernstein says, they learn different roles in their respective families: 'Children who have access to different speech systems or codes, that is children who learn different roles by virtue of their family's class position in a society' (p. 145). Working-class children would be limited to the restricted code because in their generally status-oriented families the definition of roles would be rigid. On the other hand, middle-class children could have access to the elaborated code because in their generally person-oriented families the role system would be supple: 'The ascribed status of the member, for many activities, would be weakened by his achieved status' (p. 153); 'In such a family the child learns to *make* his role rather than this being formally assigned to him' (p. 154). The notion of role has therefore nothing to do with the place assigned one in the universe of dominance relations of age, sex or class, a place which none the less prescribes one's language practices. Since the concept of role is vaguely defined, it can be advantageously used to account for some unexpected results, which pose problems to sociologists.[6]

In fact, the concept of role, borrowed from social psychology, has the function of *masking* the existence of hierarchic relations by referring the concrete experience of power relations, which alone give meaning to verbal as well as motor behaviour, to an interaction between equivalent elements of the same collectivity, 'individuals': 'Individuals come to learn their social roles through the process of communication' (p. 144). Thus it is no great surprise that Bernstein's attention, at the start centred on the social classes, quickly focuses on the family environment. Certainly, he is aware that he is abandoning something of fundamental importance:

> There is a danger to such an analysis, because it appears to separate the communication structure from the power relationships of society but this can be avoided if the same analysis can show the relationships between class structures and communication structure — which is where we began (p. 249).

However, not only did Bernstein undertake the study of socialization forms within the family only because his first correlations seemed 'crude' to him ('Indeed, even the relationship between codes and social class was seen as contingent' (p. 243)); but further, as has been seen, his analyses never deal with the entire society, with the social structure as a whole.

Voluntarism goes hand in hand with psychologism. Bernstein seems to think that school could change things 'by operating directly on the speech itself'. He feels that the function of educational institutions is to be 'faced with the problem of encouraging children to change and extend the way they normally use language. In terms of this paper, this becomes a switch from restricted to elaborated codes' (p. 163). But a school's action may concern a minority of children at the most, those whom Bernstein himself describes as already in a situation of social ascent. Under the circumstances the author reasons like a representative of the class for whose benefit schools function, a class which considers itself as an active force which can orient the course of history, which can choose and preserve or reject certain linguistic forms.

In his study of public language and formal language, Bernstein maintained: 'The problem would seem to be to preserve *public* language usage', as if this preservation (the term again denotes reification of language practices) depended on the decision of a social group, whichever it may be. Moreover this (illusory) omnipotence did seem to cause Bernstein some problems with his conscience'[7]

> Values are transmitted in any educational situation, but in this case of deliberate rational modification of experience we must be very sure that the new dimension of relevance made available does not also involve that loss of self-respect engendered by measuring human worth on a scale of occupational achievement.

In this, Bernstein can be sure that the 'evil' has already been done; for a long time now, the dominated classes have shared an ideology which imposes on each individual the idea that one *is* what one *has*.

Most of Bernstein's critics nevertheless share his opinion on the issue of school. It is considered an institution capable of transforming from within its ways of functioning. Otherwise why talk of the 'failings' of the educational system after admitting it to be an institution at the service of one class? This is to consider school as an institution whose task it is to correct social inequalities; to suggest that the school system should take into account socially devalorized language practices, which it is precisely meant to penalize, is to confuse explicit ideology and the system's actual function. It implies that the dominant class should be willing to renounce the particular form of power conferred by a certain use of language. It is not a question of machiavellianism: schools can select an 'élite' on the basis of verbal behaviours interpreted as signs of intelligence only to the extent that dominant ideology can impose itself over everyone including teachers (and sociologists . . .) who recognize it and fight it in its explicit form. Selective processes are not the conscious deliberate workings of the system's agents, whatever their desire to change or preserve it. These opinions about the role of schools are the result of idealistic conceptions which contradict the basic hypothesis: how could the school system change the type of speech without simultaneously changing the 'situations', the living conditions and the system of the symbolic interpretation of reality as a whole.

In fact Bernstein abstracts on the one hand the economic aspect and on the other the linguistic aspect from social reality as a whole. When he refers to 'material conditions', he does not define them as elements of a *social relationship*. For this reason, although he consciously grants them a determining role in the existence of linguistic codes, he ends up by 'forgetting' them in his research approach, since he centres it on an internal analysis of the linguistic data. However, by employing this type of analysis, Bernstein has raised a fundamental problem: how does each code, carrying a body of privileged meanings, play a determining role in the formation of identity? Indeed he always trips on the same stumbling-block in his search for the answer, since he studies each code in itself and each class in itself.

107

Power relations, language and identification processes
Bernstein's research on the role of language in the processes of social identification will be analysed in reference to the study whose results have been presented in Chapter 3. The study in question, resulting from the realization that comparisons based on the degrees of formal coherence are insufficient, presented a new theoretical approach to the facts of language: power relations operate within speech itself, they give meaning to the forms present as well as to those absent in each 'code', and define the system of their oppositions; in this way one can gather not just the *formal* coherence but the *discursive* coherence which exists both in dominant and in dominated speech. Bernstein took pains to show the essential role language plays in the formation of identity; but when he talks of *social* identity, he means *personal* identity. However, the fact that it really is a question of social identity can be seen by relying on history once again. It is the dominant class which has gradually assigned each one 'his/her' place, both within and through its scientific discourse on man.

Meaning is created at every historical moment   Doubtless, if Bernstein had been aware of linguistic changes in time he would have realized that class languages slowly took shape as an expression and instrument of social hierarchy in the making. During the whole of the nineteenth century the bourgeoisie forged its class identity and gradually defined itself as 'subject', inasmuch as its practices as a whole, including its language practices, allotted to the dominated social categories an identity as objects. Scientific discourse on man has not escaped the grasp of the ideology secreted by the class in power. The breaking up of reality effectuated by the social sciences is no neutral activity: knowledge about man constituted itself by progressively accentuating the categorization and hierarchization of human beings. A group of signifiers (for example 'Aryan' and 'Semitic' languages) and their syntactic organization progressively divided reality according to a system of similarities and differences, expressing and recreating at every instant concrete dominance relations.

Bernstein knows the evils of this ideology at a conscious level since he criticizes the theory of linguistic 'deficit', but is subjected to it at an unconscious level when his own theory explaining the dissimilarities in language practices does not escape it either. And yet the discourse of the social sciences is Truth in his eyes: 'Restricted codes draw upon metaphor, whereas elaborated codes draw upon rationality' (p. 176); 'The meta-languages of public forms of thought as these apply to objects and persons realize meanings of a universalistic type' (p. 175). His belief in science leads him to confuse forms of thought which are universal (universalistic) and forms of thought which are universalizing (that is to say which relate to the universalistic illusion).

The 'I', an asociological instance? Failing to recognize that power relations are expressed and are reinforced by the linguistic instrument itself, Bernstein encounters certain interpretative difficulties which lead him to fall back on psychological preconceptions. The importance of certain facts does not escape him. He notes that the dominant class's speech is 'person orientated' and centred on the speaker's person: 'The middle-class groups use a higher proportion of the pronoun "I" to total selected personal pronouns' (p. 106); on the other hand he remarks that: 'The working-class groups use "you" and "they" more frequently' (p. 107) and that their language remains impersonal even when the statement relates to the speaker's subjectivity. These facts as a whole seem obscure to Bernstein but only a part of them cause him problems: not the presence of 'I' among some, but its absence amongst others, as if the personalized form, centred on the person, were the normal form whose course all speech should follow: 'The constraint on the use of "I" is not easy to understand' (p. 110); 'Why should the unique meaning of the person be implicit rather than verbally explicit?' (p. 146).

However, Bernstein does allude to 'low level supervisory functions, where persons are often treated as objects' (p. 165); but he does not see the connection between concrete social relations (exercise of domination, subjection to domination) and social relations as symbolized in speech (elaborated code/restricted code). To perceive this connection he would first have to become decentred in relation to the ideology through which his class defines identity. Bernstein's use of the concept of identity always relates to one and the same conception of society and social relations. Sometimes he speaks of cultural identity (in the anthropological sense of the word culture), with the idea that society is homogeneous; at other times, he refers to class identity (sub-culture), but, as has been seen, each class is a self-existing system in his view; finally, the idea of personal identity, which he expresses at times, is based on a vision of society as a collection of individuals, each one a self-enclosed mini-system.

The concept of identity is not a sociological one for Bernstein. He sees the process of identification as a psychological process of 'personality' formation within the family and the class. It is therefore hardly astonishing that the concept of identity is only used to refer to the class using the elaborated code:

> On this view an educationally induced change of code from a restricted code (object) to an elaborated code (person) involves a shift in organizing concepts from authority/piety towards one of identity: from an organizing concept which makes irrelevant the question of

personal identity to an organizing concept which places the notion of identity in the forefront of the personality (p. 165).

Nevertheless whatever a child's class, he does gradually make the distinction between the 'me' and 'others'. But the point is to know precisely whence this much-talked-of 'me' takes its source. Denying that concrete relations of power have an influence on the formation of identity, the dominant class has formulated the idea of 'personality', of personal identity, to define itself, to express the vision it has of itself as a collection of 'I's, of free and responsible individuals. This is a disincarnated, asociological conception of social relations, whereas, through its use of concrete power, and also of language, this class creates a mass of undifferentiated beings which it rejects into the sphere of impersonal things, of objects. 'By identity', writes Bernstein, 'I simply mean a preoccupation with the question of "who am I?" '; but only the dominant ask this question, as the dominated have to ask the question in these terms: 'who/what am I?'

That the elaborated code, which the dominant use, contains and perpetuates their vision of themselves (as Bernstein's results show) is no surprise: 'An elaborated code, through its regulation, induces in its speakers a sensitivity to the implications of separateness and differences'; 'An elaborated code will arise wherever the culture or sub-culture emphasizes the "I" over the "we" ' (p. 147). The surprising thing is that Bernstein, who analyses the elaborated code so well, does not perceive its meaning, any more than he perceives that of the restricted code when he writes: 'The working-class children are more likely to select pronouns as heads (especially third-person pronouns)' (p. 167). He comes to hierarchize language practices precisely because differentiation of the 'me', the assertion of 'I', seems to him to be the culminating point in the history of individuals and of the human species; once the validity of this culminating point is accepted, the elaborated code can indeed be declared superior to the restricted code and one could wish that the working classes would develop relations which are more individualized, less communalist — in Bernstein's eyes, the conditions for access to the elaborated code.

Bernstein regrets that the restricted code does not give rise to 'a need to create speech which uniquely fits the intentions of the speakers. Restricted codes do not give rise to verbally differentiated "I"s' (p. 147). However, he inverts cause and effect. Although he observes that adolescents, prisoners, and the working classes (categories socially deprived of power) all use the restricted code, he does not see that dominant speech and practices impose on certain social categories an identity which calls for the same type of speech. Some of Labov's results are just as important in this connection, since, by revealing the variety of behaviours according to age and sex within the same social class, they give rise to the supposition that linguistic 'choices' depend on multiple social hierarchies, whose concrete supports are the speakers.[8]

The sole referent of all speech   Some of the results which remain obscure to Bernstein reveal their significance as soon as they are analysed according to the hypothesis that the forms used in each social sphere have something to do with concrete power relationships and their articulation in speech. As was seen in Chapter 3, if one compares the way social classes use proper and common nouns, articles, personal pronouns, adverbs and possessive pronouns, one observes that, although unconscious, the 'choices' are not arbitrary.

This explains a fact which caused Bernstein some problems: the relative absence of the pronoun 'I' in the speech of the dominated. Since only the members of the dominant class define themselves as 'person', as 'subject', and since grammatically 'I' represents the person, then 'I' has the dominant social group as referent.

According to Bernstein, the restricted code expresses and creates solidarity, 'the feeling of us to the detriment of me'. But the fact that dominated categories by their language practices define themselves as collective, as a plurality, and thereby echo the experience of power practices inflicted on them, can consequently no longer be mistaken for the expression of solidarity. In fact, for 'we' to be stated and enacted as a collection of 'I's, a set of 'subjects', a social situation must exist in which a relative control of dominant practices is possible. The fact that the dominated all experience the same situation of oppression and 'speak themselves' accordingly does not necessarily mean that there is solidarity or a feeling of 'us'. What the utterances of the dominated usually state is that they belong to a collective *object*, to an *impersonal* plurality ('as for us *lot*'). In contrast, just because speakers of the dominant class individually consider themselves as purely singular, this does not mean that their practices are individual; they are collective, for they are objectively interdependent in their power practices and in the defence of their class interests.

Dominant discourse assigns each person a definition of his/her social identity according to his/her position in the structure of dominance relationships. One of its forms of expression is precisely the code elaborated, and perpetually re-elaborated, to justify domination. The elaborated code helps to negate the everyday concrete violence of relations of exploitation by relegating the dominated to the sphere of not-quite-human. The dominant create a 'personality' for themselves by imposing on the dominated symbolic marks of the 'difference' which repels them towards a negative and impersonal pole. To this extent, Bernstein is right in writing: 'An elaborated code in principle presupposes a sharp boundary or gap between self and others which is crossed through the creation of speech which specifically fits a differentiated "other" ' (p. 147). But a differentiated 'other' does not necessarily mean a person. So the rest of his point cannot be accepted without reserve: 'In this sense an elaborated code is orientated towards a person rather than a social category or status.' If one holds that its referent is the dominant defined as a person, the elaborated code can be said to be 'orientated towards a person'. But it is not at all oriented towards a person where the dominated are concerned, since on the contrary it denies them the qualification of person and defines them only as members of a social category. Therefore, it is hardly surprising that 'a restricted code is positional or status *not* person oriented', that 'restricted codes do not give rise to verbally differentiated "I"s', for a speaker of the dominated class necessarily defines himself as part of an undifferentiated whole, of a 'generalized other'. Once again, it is regrettable that Bernstein gives such ethnocentric interpretations to his judicious observations.

The restricted and elaborated codes express class knowledge on the social relationships, but it is a class delusion to declare that the dominant class's knowledge is truer:

> Where codes are elaborated, the socialized has more access to the grounds of his own socialization, and so can enter a reflexive relationship to the social order he has taken over. Where codes are restricted, the socialized has less access to the grounds of his socialization, and thus reflexiveness may be limited in range (p. 176).

Nevertheless, is not the knowledge of the dominated class – in which the notion of 'person' poses problems – sociologically closer to reality than that of the representatives of the dominant class, who see their behaviour as a pure expression of their subjectivity? Which does not mean that the dominated are, as Bernstein believes, 'more likely to be concerned with object processes than interpersonal and intrapersonal processes' (p. 166).

It has been seen that the scientific discourse does not avoid the presuppositions of dominant ideology even when it is trying to take its distance from the latter. Despite everything, Bernstein's work marks an important step in critical thought. Certain researchers who sought to break radically with prenotions, such as Bourdieu and Passeron in France, used Bernstein's work to illustrate their theories, while insisting on the importance of cultural factors in scholastic success. However, it will be seen that they do not really overthrow the traditional approach either, and that they fall into the same errors which they denounce in others.

Notes

1 Bernstein's work has been widely circulated in France since the publication of a book entitled *Langage et classes sociales. Codes socio-linguistiques et contrôle social*, Paris, Ed. de Minuit, 1975. This work includes most of the texts published in *Class, Codes and Control*, vol. I, *Theoretical Studies Towards a Sociology of Language*, London, Routledge & Kegan Paul, 1974. As the first chapter, Basil Bernstein included his study on public and formal languages which appeared in 1961 under the title 'Social class and linguistic development. A theory of social learning', in A. H. Halsey, J. Floud, C. A. Anderson (eds), *Education, Economy and Society*, New York, Free Press, 1965. Page references are to *Class, Codes and Control*.

2 In fact, we are dealing here with stereotypes, and not with the results of an analysis of social relations in the working classes: the picture of an idyllic world without conflicts or vendettas.

3 William Labov, 'The Logic of Non-standard English', in *Language and Social Context*, Pier Paolo Giglioli (ed.), Harmondsworth, Penguin 1972 (pp. 179–215). According to Labov, it is not that the question of 'complexity' is solved any better by those who analyse language according to its 'deep structure', since they set as an absolute standard *their* order of transformation. Not only do linguists generalize on the basis of their own utterances (the utterances belonging to their class), but they cannot even agree on the grammaticality of their linguistic forms.

4 Colette Guillaumin, *L'Idéologie raciste. Genèse et langage actuel*, Paris, Mouton, 1971.

5 An evolutionistic view underlies this statement: the working classes are supposed to have remained at the level of the restricted code because their social relationships would still be of the mechanic solidarity type.

6 Thus, as Henderson's results seem to show, it is because they have highly differentiated 'roles' that the eldest *daughters* of big working-class families have a superior ability to manipulate language. Similarly, the differentiation of masculine and feminine 'roles' is supposed to modulate the correlation between belonging to the working classes and using the restricted code: 'For various reasons, in particular the occupation of the mother before marriage and the role differentiation within the family, there will not be a one-to-one correlation between the use of a restricted code and the working-class stratum, but the probability is certainly very high' (p. 91). In this case, the problem of a married woman's class belonging and thus of class definition causes Bernstein problems, as it does many other sociologists (C. Delphy admirably demonstrated the logical aberrations which authors of studies on social mobility are reduced to; C. Delphy, 'Les femmes dans les études de stratification', in A. Michel (ed.), *Femmes, sexisme et sociétés*, Paris, PUF,

1977). Indeed, the sentence implies that the mother of a working-class family does not necessarily use the restricted code (but that she is none the less categorized as belonging to the working-class because of her husband's occupation). If the occupation she had before marriage (one does not know what happens if she has an occupation after marriage) meant that she used the elaborated code, which could only be acquired in a non-working-class family, would a mother's social origin then define her class?

7   The quotation refers to page 309 of the text which appeared in Halsey *et al.*

8   William Labov, 'The study of language in its social context' in *Advances in Sociology of Language*, Joshua Fishman (ed.), Paris, Mouton, 1971, pp. 152--216.

5 Shortcomings in the theory of the 'unequal distribution of linguistic capital'

In 1945, a criticism of the theory of natural aptitudes was undertaken in France by P. Naville,[1] who analysed its justificative function in his *Théorie de l'orientation professionnelle*. But the social sciences resumed this critique only in the 1960s. At the time, confronted with problems concerning the numeric growth of schoolgoers at all levels of teaching, as well as what is known as the teaching 'crisis', the sociology of education began to examine the practices of scholastic selection using the same perspective as Naville had done for the practices of occupational selection and orientation.

Compared to the Anglo-American sociology of the time, critical sociology started to take on a novel aspect in France with the works of J. C. Passeron and P. Bourdieu. In the wake of Bernstein, whose first works they considered 'remarkable', they examined the linguistic factors which condition school success and the different classes' chances of access to higher education. But contrary to their precursor, their approach to classes made an explicit break with traditional American sociology and its view of a stratified homogeneous society.[2] Although in their first works, they talked of 'lower classes', 'disadvantaged classes', 'upper classes', they then adopted a terminology, i.e. 'dominated classes' and 'dominant classes', taken from the class theory which seemed to them the most fruitful: that of Marx. They nevertheless availed themselves of Weber's and Durkheim's contributions, borrowing elements from the former for the object of their study, symbolic imposition, and from the latter his knowledge of the field, the educational system.

The work, entitled *Reproduction in Education, Society and Culture*,[3] presents a synthesis of their studies in the sociology of education and stipulates with great precision the theoretical foundations of their analysis: the function of school is to contribute to social reproduction, that is, according to their definition, to 'the reproduction of the structure of the relations of force between the classes' (p. 11). Criticizing in Durkheim 'the implicit premiss that the different pedagogic actions at work in a social formation collaborate harmoniously in reproducing a cultural capital conceived of as the jointly owned property of the whole "society" ' (p. 11), the authors of the book specify that:

> In reality, because they correspond to the material and symbolic
> interests of groups or classes differently situated within the power
> relations, these pedagogic actions always tend to reproduce the
> structure of the distribution of cultural capital among these groups
> or classes, thereby contributing to the reproduction of the social
> structure (p. 11).

However, they wished to qualify and to complete the classical materialist approach:

> Marx concerned to reveal the relations of violence underlying the
> ideologies of legitimacy, tends in his analysis of the effects of the
> dominant ideology to minimize the real efficacy of the symbolic
> strengthening of power relations (*rapports de force*) that is implied
> in the recognition by the dominated of the legitimacy of domination
> ... (p. 5).

For this reason, they centred their analysis on the study of the purely
pedagogic mechanisms through which symbolic violence is used in its
different forms.

On the level of the processes, the outline of what is proposed by the
authors is as follows: each class, given its position in the structure of
power relationships, selects a body of meanings and thus shapes a
specific 'habitus' for itself, i.e. 'common schemes of thought, perception, appreciation and action' (p. 35). Subjected from the start to the
cultural arbitrary of a family environment which instils them with their
class 'habitus', children are then confronted with the cultural arbitrary
of the school system, which is none other than that of the dominant
class. When the younger generations are successively subjected to different pedagogic actions, they are not aware of being subjected to symbolic
violence, because in their eyes their parents and teachers are invested
with a pedagogic authority which confers legitimacy on their *de facto*
power. Thus the system can reproduce itself with the unconscious
complicity of the social agents who 'interiorize' the structures and
regulate their behaviour according to the implicit knowledge they have
of the possibilities objectively offered them by the social system. Therefore school can accomplish its function of perpetuating power relationships, because it does so without anybody realizing it:

> the traditional system of education manages to present the illusion
> that its action of inculcation is [. . .] independent of class determin-
> ations — whereas it tends towards the limit of merely confirming and
> strengthening a class habitus which, constituted outside the School,
> is the basis of all scholastic acquirements (p. 205).

Since school exerts a dominant pedagogic action, based on the 'habitus' of the dominant class, it follows that education is a process of acculturization for children of the dominated classes, who have fewer trumps in hand to succeed in their studies. For Passeron and Bourdieu, differential success according to class depends on two factors: 'the pedagogic ethos' and 'the cultural capital' appropriate to each class (p. 30). What is pedagogic ethos? It is a system of dispositions to school which is defined as the product of the internalization of the value which school accords previous family education. As for cultural capital, it is the 'cultural goods' transmitted by the family, and its value depends on the distance between the cultural arbitrary imposed by the dominant pedagogic action and the cultural arbitrary inculcated within the different groups or classes (p. 30).

This summary of an approach which Passeron and Bourdieu have developed throughout their work is intended to give an idea of novelty and import in the sociology of education. They broadened the scope of a theoretical debate which had previously often been reduced to pragmatic consideration dictated by the school institution itself. The cult of school did not stand up to a critical inspection carried out from inside the institution by two of its representatives.

Nevertheless, as will be seen, Passeron and Bourdieu's attempt to upset the existing perspectives remains incomplete. As agents of the school system, they have had a tendency to carry out a purely internal analysis of this institution, without examining its relation to the economic system. Forgetting, when they criticized the ideology of the 'gift', the importance of P. Naville's contribution which had shown that the theory of aptitudes narrowly corresponded to the requirements of a specific economic system, they came to treat the school system not as if it were relatively autonomous but as completely independent. Whereas *concrete* and not just *symbolic* dominance relations constitute social classes and sex classes into antagonistic groups, they tended to favour the symbolic aspect. With the viewpoint that differences in scholastic success are based on power relationships between the classes as their starting point, the authors then discarded precisely these power relationships in their empirical studies.

Failure to recognize the relationship between economic power and knowledge

Anxious to dissociate themselves from the image of a Marxist based research reduced to primary materialism (in the first publication of their study of 'cultural heritage', they wrote: 'the conversion of cultural heritage into social heritage is not restricted to the influence of material conditions'), Passeron and Bourdieu focused principally on symbolic aspects. But, in their empirical research, they ended up by 'forgetting' and thus masking the fact that economic power is a condition for the appropriation of institutionalized knowledge.

Of course they are right to emphasize that the educational system's relative autonomy rules out the possibility of considering it no more than a pure 'reflection' of a specific aspect of the economic system and a mere tool designed to adapt, as technocrats would have it, individuals to the employment market:

> So it has to be asked whether the freedom the educational system is given to enforce its own standards and its own hierarchies, at the expense for example of the most evident demands of the economic system, is not the quid pro of the hidden services it renders to certain classes by concealing social selection under the guise of technical selection . . . (p. 153).

This is a relevant criticism, which insists on the ideological function of the educational system. But does this necessarily mean that one should discard the problem of the relation between the economic system and the educational system? Page after page, the authors repeatedly state that it is the structure of class relationships which is the ultimate basis for scholastic inequalities. But what, in concrete terms, do these relationships mean to them, how do they integrate them in their analysis of selection processes?

Economic power or 'income'?
In their empirical work, not only do the authors turn a blind eye to the economic reality because they give preference to ideological factors, but when they refer to the economic aspect they are no longer speaking of power relations or domination. They use notions such as 'material conditions', 'social conditions', 'conditions of existence' which henceforth form a part of all scientific discourse on school and whose only function is to draw attention away from the social relationships, from the dominance relationships between the classes and the sexes. If one refers to their empirical studies, the authors define class belonging by means of 'the conditions of existence', 'ethos', 'cultural capital'; as for social sex, it is labelled 'demographic characteristic' (p. 255). At first, it would seem that this is in contradiction to their theoretical stand-point (power relationships between classes) but contradiction is nothing less than apparent, for, in fact, they reduce economic power to income, i.e. the material quantity of money which each family disposes of.

In their study, first published under the title *Rapport pédagogique et communication*[3] which now constitutes Chapter 1 of *Reproduction*, they uncritically employ the results of a study by P. Clerc:

Mr. P. Clerc has succeeded in demonstrating that with equal diplomas, income (strongly linked, as one knows, to the education
level of the head of family) exerts no influence on scholastic success
and that, quite on the contrary, with equal income, the proportion
of good pupils grows in a systematically significant manner depending on whether the father has no diploma or has the baccalauréat,
which enables one to conclude that the influence of family environment on scholastic success is, at the moment, almost exclusively
cultural (p. 55).

It seems curious that one can postulate as equally true two such
problem-raising assertions: on the one hand, it is asserted that income is
strongly linked to the level of education, on the other hand one declares
that only the parents' level of education bears an influence on the
children's scholastic success. The entire sophism of the reasoning, which
is blind to the contradiction, arises from forgetting the first assertion.
Indeed, one no longer takes anything into consideration other than the
well-nigh empty spaces of the correlation table: education level X
income, which gives the following reasoning: since the child of a lycée
graduate manual worker has as much chance of success as the child of
a lycée graduate company director, one can conclude that income has no
real influence on success. In any case, one cannot avoid a vicious circle:
the acquisition of knowledge presupposes the acquisition of knowledge.

To reduce economic power to an 'income' which in itself could or
could not be a determining factor in scholastic success indicates a failure
to recognize the fact that knowledge has become one of the dimensions
of economic power, and that, in a social formation in which the economic dimension embraces everything in its type of rationality, ideological power is invested with a specific force (since being is defined, as
has been seen, by having).

As Establet and Baudelot pointed out in criticism,[4] Passeron and
Bourdieu made generalizations, about the entire educational system on
the basis of analyses referring to one of its levels, higher education, and
to one particular sector, *Lettres*. Fascinated by the analysis of the type
of traditional education they were subject to and which the institution
forced them in turn to inculcate as teachers, they tend to represent it as
the whole of knowledge. Where the perpetuation of the university system
and its contribution to the perpetuation of power relationships between
the classes are concerned, everything seems to suggest that the dominant
class keeps itself in power by transmitting to its inheritors a knowledge
which all in all is artificial: 'the relation of pedagogic communication
can perpetuate itself even when the information transmitted tends
towards zero' (p. 107). Of course we know that the game is worth it,
for this knowledge can be cashed in on, it is a source of power, like the

119

knowledge of sorcerers and priests (social agents whose practices are often used to illustrate statements relating to the agents of the educational system; however, the analogy, though attractive from a literary point of view, often serves in scientific discourse to conceal an experiment's lack of rigour).

Having failed to analyse the new dimension assumed by institutionalized knowledge, Passeron and Bourdieu tended to reduce it to a purely distinctive sign of class; they would have its effectiveness depend solely on a class's power to impose its 'cultural arbitrary' by imposing the recognition of its power's legitimacy. But nowadays knowledge has become something more than a 'salon culture', a flourish of knowledge, education something more than an initiation rite. Scientific and technical knowledge do not have the same function as literary knowledge and worldly know-how, to which the authors always seem to refer. A knowledge-tool also exists on which relations of economic dominance are founded: theoretical and practical knowledge have become necessary means for the enlarged reproduction of capital. What is more, in its application, this knowledge helps reinforce the ideology of aptitudes in a new way, for it appears to all as a source of 'progress', including to critical sociologists who state: 'the progress of the division of labour entailing the autonomization of intellectual tribunals or practices . . .' (p. 55), as though they did not realize that the ideological notion of progress negates relations of exploitation on which the autonomization of intellectual practices rests.

Economic constraints
Everything induces us to find that Bourdieu and Passeron see only 'symbolic violence' in the mechanisms of selection, as though they ignored that relations of economic dominance *also* fundamentally determine scholastic options and success.

When one knows that dominant-class families invest a considerably less important part of their capital in the intellectual education of their daughters than in that of their sons, when one knows that this form of inequality in the actual right to the economic heritage serves the purpose of perpetuating economic dominance relationships between the sexes, can one then reduce the mechanisms of the appropriation of knowledge to the sphere of 'symbolic violence'? One only has to re-read Virginia Woolf (*The Three Guineas*) to ascertain that submission, internalization of objective chances and elimination of the self are not the only mechanisms at work: the dominant respond to an acute awareness of the perfectly concrete power relations depriving the dominated of a socially profitable knowledge-tool, of concrete possibilities of economic independence as well as of all power, with practices which are far from symbolic.

It is also known that a great proportion of dominant-class children escape being eliminated from school thanks to private schools, a system of parallel education whose extremely expensive services allow this class to refuse the verdicts of a school alleged for all. Furthermore, it is not by pure chance that *écoles normales d'instituteurs* (French teacher training colleges), which pay their pupils' fees and living expenses, take the most 'brilliant' pupils of the dominated class. Mere habitus, class ethos, or submission to certain economic imperatives? At any rate, analysis of the opinions of students whom this choice has been forced upon reveals that they are not entirely fooled by the ideology of the 'gift' for in their eyes scholastic success is above all a 'question of money'; it is for the privileged that it becomes solely a 'question of environment'.

It should be remembered that at the time when Passeron and Bourdieu took the cultural practices of *Lettres* students as an object of study, the majority of students issuing from the economically dominated class had a paid job to ensure their material subsistence during their studies (see Chapter 2). In Paris, in 1962–3, the year in which the authors carried out their studies, this was the case of 80 per cent of those who, after a year, had to give up their plans to obtain an advanced teaching diploma. However, Bourdieu and Passeron defined their object of study in such a way that these facts inevitably escaped their attention: their object was not the social classes (of which they would be analysing the power relations in those institutions where one acquires knowledge), but 'the differential reception of the pedagogic message' differentiating the classes. Therefore, for them, the problem of scholastic success was reduced to a problem of the success of pedagogic communication. Thus, they were only interested in students who underwent their pedagogic action while attending professiorial courses. They excluded from the field in which knowledge is at stake, all wage-earning students originating from the dominated class who did not have the actual possibility of attending courses and who based their intellectual learning on reading and compulsory attendance to a few practical exercises. The problem of acquiring a diploma concerned these students too, whereas the pedagogic game concerned only the most privileged section. By restricting their definition of student to those who received the professorial message orally, the authors made the mistake of thinking that any student, whatever his/her class of origin, is defined solely by his immediate relation to the institution (they were not concerned with his/her position in the economic system). Precisely because of this, they failed to gather data which would have led them to examine the weight of economic constraints on scholastic success.

After all, one might consider that the sociology of education is indebted to the authors for their brilliant analyses of the subtleties of the pedagogic game. Nevertheless, it is necessary to underline that their choice of population could only give a partial view of the processes at work in university selection, which constitutes the central theme of their considerations. The consequences are not without importance, for in their research practice, they omitted an element which is none the less fundamental to their theory, 'material conditions'.[5] Since they explained scholastic success through purely cultural factors, the question remains to know whether in their opinion the exercise of an economic activity is a 'cultural' fact.

This cannot be ruled out. Indeed, as is current in the social sciences, Passeron and Bourdieu use the word culture in its anthropological sense without perceiving the term's polysemia. Indeed, this word includes under one and the same heading practices which sociological analysis should distinguish with all due rigour. Is it logically and sociologically relevant to liken *leisure* practices (going to the theatre, the cafés, Saturday-night dances) to *productive* practices, whether of goods or of services, which constitute a social work (e.g. working in a vegetable garden, carrying a baby on one's back or on one's arm while cultivating yams or transporting the family group's food, etc.)? This assimilation of leisure practices with practices which present a real economic interest results in hiding the fact that it is the dominant group's (class and sex) interests which are at stake and that the possibility of abandoning oneself to leisure practices is not offered equally to all.

Early on, and this is important if one does not try to exclude the problem of the relation between the economic system and the scholastic system from the analysis of the processes of scholastic selection, the children of the dominated class are economic agents producing services *as well as* schoolchildren, especially if they are of the female sex. Who benefits from this work, which is not remunerated yet socially necessary (as is all domestic work carried out by women and forgotten in economic calculations), if not the dominant class as a whole and the male population as a whole? The fact of assuming different 'roles' (as social psychologists put it), or more precisely of working, is a constraint imposed by economic dominance relations which are at the basis of depriving the dominated of socially profitable knowledge.

Thus in Bourdieu and Passeron's empirical work, one of the points which seemed fundamental in the claims of their theoretical assertions, 'power relations', is rapidly excluded from the analysis of selection processes, which in fact is limited to the analysis of the processes of inculcation of dominant 'culture' and of the dominant class's language. It was necessary to underline what had remained unsaid, and maybe unknown, in a discourse which insisted on dominance relationships: incantatory references to 'power relations' cannot indeed be passed off as an analysis. If there are no purely physical power relationships, as the authors state, neither is there any violence which is merely symbolic. A proto-Marxist, culturalist discourse, *Reproduction*, did not overthrow previous perspectives as the authors had hoped.

However, it has been seen that the fact that power relationships were put into parentheses in Bernstein's analyses did not prevent him from collecting extremely interesting data on the differential linguistic practices of the social classes. Consequently, it is necessary to examine the importance of the results of Bourdieu and Passeron's work in the field in which they restricted their study: the unequal distribution of linguistic capital between the classes.

'Linguistic capital' or proof through the absence of facts

The hypothesis which Passeron and Bourdieu wished to verify through their empiric work, the results of which are presented in Chapter 1 of their book, is as follows:

> the academic market value of each individual's linguistic capital is a
> function of the distance between the type of symbolic mastery
> demanded by the School and the practical mastery he owes to his
> initial class upbringing (primary pedagogical work) (p. 116).

> The influence of linguistic capital, particularly manifest in the first
> years of schooling [. . .] never ceases to be felt (p. 73).

Such are the hypotheses to be verified. The authors advise those interested in the scientific aspect of the demonstration, in the modalities used in putting facts to the test, to refer to the study's original text (*Rapport pédagogique et communication*), which was published in 1965. Indeed, it has the advantage of indicating the population, the locality, the type of tests which served to produce the results commented on in *Reproduction*.

Collecting the data
In 1962–3, a population of 496 students of philosophy and sociology from Paris and eleven other towns were submitted to tests on the comprehension and manipulation of words belonging to scholarly language. Five types of exercises were given to them:

1 To spot words used incorrectly in a statement, e.g. 'incunable' (incunabulum), 'tératologie' (teratology), 'prodrome' (prodrome), 'névropathe' (neuropath) . . .
2 To define five words pertaining mostly to the philosophical vocabulary: 'antinomie' (antinomy), 'cadastre' (cadastre), 'épistémologie' (epistemology), 'extension − d'un concept −'

(extension — of a concept —), 'manichéisme' (Manichaeanism).
3 Polysemia: to seek all the possible meanings of certain words: 'attribut' (attribute), 'fonction' (function), 'image' (image) . . . .
4 Knowledge of concrete language: in a list of words, finding a synonym for: 'aîtres' (premisses), 'carrier' (quarryman), 'comparse' (confederates), 'émétique' (emetic) . . .; to choose from four possibilities the correct definition of the words: 'alésage' (broaching), 'fraisage' (drilling) . . . .
5 Knowledge of the vocabulary of the humanities: to underline the correct definition of 'contrepoint' (counterpoint), 'sonate' (sonata), 'glacis' (glaze), 'Hélène' (Helen), 'litote' (litotes) . . . .

The answers to the tests were corrected, then histograms were drawn up showing the distribution of the results according to sex, social class etc. A table recapitulating the essentials of the results enables one to compare the median of the results of different groups, whose performances are evaluated in relation to score 12 (the median of the results of the population as a whole). The reading of the median of the different groups (an index which, according to the authors themselves, has the inconvenience of masking the fact that certain repartitions are bimodal) indicates no marked differences. Maybe this is why the authors did not proceed to a significance test. In any case, they retained only one test from the body of results: the exercise on the definition of five words belonging to philosophical vocabulary (correcting this involved using the most subjective criteria as compared with the other tests).

Apart from the fact that one may consider it not very rigorous, from a scientific point of view, to choose arbitrarily from a certain number of results those on which the demonstration is to be based, one might consider that the data chosen here is rather slight to enable one to judge the linguistic performances of different categories of students, let alone the 'linguistic capital' of different classes. Whatever the case may be, let us follow, as the authors invite us to, the account of a multivariate analysis which sets out to specify how the performances of each individual vary according to his class origin, his sex, his region of origin, the type of scholastic education he received in secondary school ('classical', Latin and/or Greek, or 'modern').

What does one observe, given the hypothesis at the start? That linguistic performances do not differ according to social class, and that in some cases (e.g. working-class students from Paris) the results even tend to show that the expected relation between social origin and pedagogic success is inverted. This leads one to suppose that, at least for the students attending the course, cultural heritage has no determining effect on scholastic success. (According to my own research discussed in Chapter 2, one indeed finds the greatest proportion of graduates at the end of the advanced studies amongst students originating from the dominated class when these students *do not work* to earn a living.) Therefore, one question is raised, given Bourdieu and Passeron's results: what about the importance of cultural heritage and linguistic capital?

Interpreting the results
Right from the start, the authors warn us against an overhasty interpretation of the results: one should not interpret them without re-integrating them into the temporal processes in which they assume significance. In fact, they explain:

> Given that they have had to achieve a successful acculturation in order to meet the irreducible minimum of academic requirements as regards language, the working-class and middle-class students who reach higher education have necessarily undergone more stringent selection, precisely in terms of the criterion of linguistic competence . . . (p. 73).

The authors thus add to their first explicative principle, 'linguistic capital', a second one, 'the relative degree of selection' (over-selected, under-selected) in order to explain the levels of receptivity to the pedagogic message which students of different social classes attain at the level of higher education:

> The capacity of reception characteristic of receivers of a given category is a function at once of that category's *linguistic capital* [. . .] and the *degree of selection* of the survivors in that category, as objectively measured by the rate of elimination of that category from the educational system (p. 91).

The table showing the results of the test (very competent ++, competent +, average 0, weak −, very weak −−), called the 'linguistic competence' table and elaborated according to the number of students in each category to have got a mark higher than 12, then takes on great significance for Bourdieu and Passeron.[6] In their opinion, it is the direct result of the combined effect of linguistic capital and selection degree. Subsequently, they formed the hypothesis that a fair competence (+) could result from the combination of solid capital (++) with weak selection (−), the case of the upper classes; or conversely, of no capital (−) combined with over-selection (++); the case of children from the working classes. Thus the authors invented two more scales which they compared with the scale of language-exercise results for each category of students: that of 'degree of relative selection' (worked out with the help of statistics giving 'indication of the various subgroups' chances of university entrance'), and that of 'linguistic capital'. The latter, however, was constructed in a seemingly arbitrary manner, since each category finds itself attributed a + or a − according to criteria of evaluation which are never rendered explicit.

Moreover, one wonders whether this scale is justified. If it is obvious that the test results are distributed from + to −, since the experiment was constructed to this end, one cannot see what authorizes the authors to establish *a priori* that classes are distributed along a scale which disposes them in order of linguistic 'goods' (capital). One is now far from the view of classes as it was presented on a theoretical level; as one sees, in their empirical studies the authors have given up defining classes as antagonistic groups; they turn them into fractions of a homogeneous whole, into strata which they hierarchize according to cultural practices. This choice is all the more unexpected in so far as the data of Bernstein's studies, to which the authors have referred ever since their first works, clearly showed (in spite of the fact that Bernstein's data are confined to complexity indexes) that there exist radical qualitative, and not quantitative, differences between the verbal practices of the dominated and those of the dominant.

Furthermore, we do not know on what Bourdieu and Passeron base themselves when they declare the 'middle-class [clerical staff, craftsmen and private traders, middle management] students are as disadvantaged with respect to linguistic capital as working-class students' (p. 80). This, it seems, disregards socio-linguistic studies, which on the contrary insist on the so-called middle class's grammatical hyper-correctness. According to what, if not banal prejudices, do the authors establish *a priori* (p. 74) that the linguistic capital of Parisian school children is superior to that of provincial schoolchildren? (The test performances of students from a big provincial town such as Lyon are indeed identical to those of Parisian students, as is shown by the first published version of their results.)

Above all, we are trapped, with the authors, in a vicious circle: whereas students underwent certain tests to check the hypothesis of an unequal distribution of linguistic capital between social classes, the results of the experiments ended up by being explained by . . . the unequal distribution of linguistic capital at the start of school. Doubtless this 'mathematical' game invented for the purposes of demonstration is entertaining, but one can deplore the fact that the authors got themselves caught in this game while thinking they were doing scientific work. One cannot but agree with them when they criticize (p. 103) those who, obsessed by methodology, forget to look at the meaning of the data they manipulate. But one cannot envisage accepting the alternative they have to offer: pulling a rabbit out of the hat under the veneer of scientificity. Indeed, what else is this 'theoretical model' which proposes to add what cannot be added, which combines completely heterogeneous elements and treats presuppositions as though they were duly established facts?

Besides, not even established facts escape being subjected to a reinterpretation for the purposes of demonstration, as will be shown by analysing what the terms 'degree of relative selection' and 'overselection' imply.

Quod erat demonstrandum

Whether they are aware of it or not, Bourdieu and Passeron make use of the explicative notion of 'selection' in two different senses. They come, by means of a gradual change of meaning, to confuse second-rate with first-rate pupils. When they refer to the small minority of working-class children present at university who owe their scholastic survival to particularly outstanding successes, they are reasoning in terms of overselection. But in all cases, they postulate an equivalence between 'few' and 'élite'; they equate scarcity = value. Let us take one example among others of illogicalities which are induced by this postulate. Boys, they tell us, on the whole gave more adequate definitions of the five words in the test. By applying their interpretation system, the two sociologists arrive at this reasoning: all girls are in *Lettres*, but only a few boys are; *therefore*, more selected boys represent an 'élite' in comparison to girls; *therefore* it is logical that they have better results:

> Since we know that female students are twice as likely as male students to enrol in Arts courses [. . .] and that, compared with the men, for whom the other faculties open their doors more widely, women Arts students [. . .] are less strongly selected than the male students in the same faculty, it is understandable that their performance should be weaker (p. 77).

But does it not denote a betrayal of the facts in favour of the beauty of the argument to assert that nothing distinguishes girls from boys as far as selection for university entrance is concerned (p. 80)? Indeed, further on (p. 225) we are told that the probability of access to university (leaving aside access to the important scientific schools from which girls are practically excluded) is 61 per cent for *Professions and senior executives'* sons, but only 51·2 per cent for the daughters. Must one also recall that the degree of relative selection is far from identical precisely in those disciplines which were chosen by the authors for their study, i.e. philosophy and sociology? Ten per cent of the boys in the social sciences choose these disciplines as opposed to 5 per cent of the girls.[7]

If Bourdieu and Passeron forget such obvious facts, it is because they were convinced that, quantitatively fewer in *Lettres*, boys were consequently a 'better' product of scholastic selection. However, knowledge of the facts allows one to doubt the evidence and simplicity of their argument. For, if in *Lettres*, one observes the presence of 'brilliant' sons of academics, who, faithful to classical humanism, start university intending to graduate with the *agrégation*, one must also note that an important group of dominant-class students is what the scholastic tradition calls 'dunces'. If, taking their scholastic results into consideration, they had been able to envisage studying at an important *grande école* or in Medical or Science faculties, they would not have 'chosen *Lettres*, ranked lowest in the hierarchy of the disciplines (and consequently reserved to the female population). In fact, these sons of the dominant class, who had no other choice but to apply for *Lettres* after failing several times in private secondary schools, have rarely passed the baccalauréat with distinction and represent second-rate pupils.

It is regrettable that the empirical studies carried out by Bourdieu and Passeron to prove the relevance of their thesis are neither up to the theoretical propositions advanced, nor sufficiently rigorous for one to consider the results convincing. But even if one credits them with all the facts with which they hope to persuade the reader, the said reader still observes that the rhetoric of their discourse ill conceals its contradictions. We started from the hypothesis that the scholastic elimination of the working classes would to a great extent be due to an incomplete mastery of the scholarly language used in school. With the authors, we said at the start that 'the influence of linguistic capital never ceases to be felt'. The results of the experiment, which were supposed to lead to the confirmation of the hypothesis, in fact helped to invalidate it, since it turned out that, according to the vocabulary test, students issuing from the working classes revealed as much 'aptitude of handling scholarly language'. But that need be no obstacle, since Chapter 2 of the work later 'explains' that it is not so much what is said as the way it is said which is taken into consideration by the teaching profession:

> methodical observation of the linguistic and gestural behaviour of candidates in an oral examination enables us to bring to light some of the social signs by which professorial judgment is unconsciously guided, and among which we must count the indices of the modality of the use of language (grammar, accent, tone, delivery, etc.) . . . (p. 118).

One is certainly perfectly willing to concur, provided the existence of a correlation between 'linguistic and gestural behaviour' and scholastic success in terms of acquiring a diploma is demonstrated.

None the less, to the reader's surprise, the authors consider that they have established the correlations between social origin, linguistic capital and scholastic success, not just at the level of higher education but at all levels. The fact that the survey allowed them to establish no such correlation did not impede them from asserting: 'This survey reveals [. . .]

the determining role played by linguistic heritage in scholastic success' (*Rapport pédagogique* . . .), and 'The unequal social-class distribution of *educationally profitable linguistic capital* constitutes one of the best-hidden mediations through which the relationship (grasped by our tests) between social origin and scholastic achievement is set up' . . . (p. 116). Furthermore, some important questions remain unanswered: how did working-class students escape from the disaster which befell the great majority of the children of their class of origin? And if children of the middle classes are bereft of linguistic capital, what causes them to undergo a less severe selection? A different attitude to school (ethos)? But, in this case, did 'the relative improvement in their standard of living' (p. 103) allow the middle classes to modify their class 'ethos'? And since, despite their handicap, these categories are not eliminated as much as the working classes, should one infer that ethos can compensate for the lack of linguistic capital?

So many contradictions in a discourse, so many falsely explicative statements, so much violence done to the facts, give rise to a question. What are the authors trying to prove to themselves, and to us, what do they want to convince us of, and why? It appears, in fact, as though what impairs the logic of their scientific discourse is the force of an ideology they are not aware of and which is at work under the guise of scientificity. Is this ideology not the one which they believe they are striving against by proposing a new explicative theory?

The so-called Upper Classes

Although in their theoretical statements the authors refuse to reify cultural practices, to define classes as entities with permanent attributes, the discourse of *Reproduction* is nevertheless organized in reference to the dominant social group and, under analysis, discloses the ambiguous side of the authors' explicit declarations as far as their materialistic approach is concerned.

The social relationships: a word or an analysed reality?
Everything makes it seem as though concentrating on the dominant class's practices had stopped the authors from analysing what is really at the bottom of their thesis: the relations between classes. One only has to ask oneself about a key concept in their theory, 'linguistic capital', to observe that the idea of social relations implying oppositions between practices is absent from it.

Bourdieu and Passeron, realizing that the dominant class profits from its theoretical and practical knowledge of words and their use, imagined a market for symbolic goods and arrived at the notion of linguistic capital. But is it relevant to refer to language practices by using a concept which includes within its definition the ideas of accumulation and enlarged reproduction? Even if a knowledge of 'the' language ensures certain material benefits for a fraction of a class, it is not the accumulation of written productions or use of 'the' language *per se* which are instruments of domination. Rather, it is by the meaning it conveys that the dominant class's language becomes an efficient tool of domination, but this meaning must be readjusted perpetually to justify power *de facto*. From this point of view, one cannot talk of accumulation and reproduction, but only of reorganization which sometimes creates ruptures, as has been illustrated by the history of the notion of aptitudes. In Chapter 3, it was seen how meaning is constantly re-created and articulated through social discourse which expresses the power relationship, just as much on the dominated as on the dominant side.

However, the idea that power relations exist in language practices is alien to the concept of linguistic capital. Indeed, by establishing scales of 'linguistic competence' and of 'linguistic capital' along which they dispose the classes, Passeron and Bourdieu, as we have already noted, fall back on a theoretical approach — that of strata — which denies the idea of power relationships. When they take the 'unequal distribution of linguistic capital between the classes' as explicative principle, the authors are doing no more than reviving the old metaphor of a linguistic treasure: each social group helps itself from this treasure in an unequal manner (the authors only reproach Durkheim and the culturalists for presuming that cultural capital is the 'jointly owned property of the whole of society'). Now by treating the languages of the dominated and dominant classes as unequal fractions of a whole, as quantitatively appreciable possessions, they deviate the meaning of the concept of capital. They reduce capital to what Marx reproached bourgeois economic thinking for having done: a substance, a thing, hiding that it is a question of *social relationship*. Talking about 'the' linguistic capital, 'the' language incessantly, the authors incur the risk of reifying antagonistic social practices.

The authors' use of another fundamental explicative notion in their theory, 'cultural arbitrary', suggests that the idea of a dichotomy often takes the place of the idea of social relation. The authors stipulate the meaning they give the word 'arbitrary', defining it as what 'cannot be deduced from any universal principle, whether physical, biological or spiritual, not being linked by any sort of internal relation to the "nature of things" or any "human nature" ' (p. 8). Each class supposedly imposes its cultural arbitrary by means of its pedagogic authority (it being clearly understood that the dominant class in any case imposes its own cultural arbitrary as the only legitimate culture): 'The selection of meanings which objectively defines a group's or a class's culture as a symbolic system is sociologically *necessary* in so far as that culture owes its existence to the social conditions of which it is the product' (p. 8). But if one talks of the school institution and the family institution in the same terms: 'pedagogic authority' and 'imposition of a cultural arbitrary', one incurs the risk of confusing dominance relationships, class antagonism, and dependence relationships between generations. If one believes that each class imposes *its own* cultural arbitrary, *its own* specific pedagogic influence, one ends up by juxtaposing the practices of each and one no longer perceives the structure of the oppositions they constitute. For is it sociologically relevant to talk of 'the different forms of the accomplished man as defined by the culture of the dominated groups or classes' (p. 35)? There cannot be such a thing as an 'accomplished man' for the dominated. The hidden referent of social discourse always relates them to incompleteness, and their linguistic practices are necessarily marked by this. In the same way as there cannot be two forms of cultural arbitrary in a class society, similarly it seems absurd to define cultural arbitrary as 'a logical construct devoid of any sociological or, *a fortiori*, psychological referent' (p. 11), since concrete power relationships are expressed through antagonistic linguistic forms inevitably organized around the social referent: the group in power.

The group of reference

To talk of 'sons' while demonstrating a general proposition applying to 'sons and daughters' (e.g. pp. 6, 89), constitutes a banal logical error in sociology, but it is astonishing in a case where the majority of the population studied is of the feminine sex. The referent is not only sexed, but also 'class-ified'; the use of the term 'upper classes', moreover, sums up perfectly well the authors' real ambiguity: on the one hand, they refer to the Marxist approach of the classes (power relationships, etc.), but on the other hand, they cling to the essentialist ideology revealed by the impossibility of apprehending the upper classes without attributing to them an intrinsic superiority.

Of course, according to the authors, the dominant class could only shape its culture, its language, because it benefited from certain material conditions; conditions which each generation continues to benefit from: 'the pre-school or para-school education that is given anonymously by the conditions of existence . . .' (p. 218). But when they tell us that children of the working classes do not benefit from the 'same changes' we see that this implies a reference to those favoured by chance, i.e. at the top of the social hierarchy; we are far from the idea of power relationships. The word 'chance' is important if one wishes to understand what the authors' questioning of the relations between school and the structure of power relationships consists of. It is close to the ideological approach of social mobility and strata:

> the structure of the objective chances of social upgrading according
> to class of origin and, more precisely, the structure of the chances of
> upgrading through education, conditions agents' dispositions towards
> education and towards upgrading through education — dispositions
> which in turn play a determining role in defining the [. . .] likeli-
> hood of social upgrading (p. 156).

Once again, this means reducing the dominance relationships at work in
the acquisition of knowledge to the level of a huge individual competition.

The use of the words 'chances of access' and 'ascent' is not insignifi-
cant. Bourdieu and Passeron thereby indicate that the top, the dominant
class, is the referent of their discourse, and this is not without being
connected to the idea that this class has attained a superior level of
development: 'through all the skill-learning processes of everyday life,
and particularly through the acquisition of the mother tongue [. . .]
logical dispositions are mastered in their practical state. These dispositions, more or less complex, more or less elaborated symbolically,
depending on the group or class . . .' (p. 43). Once again, of course, we
are reminded that it is materially and not biologically that children of
the dominated class are impeded in the development of their aptitudes,
but, notwithstanding, they are considered incapable of logical mastery:
'the material conditions of their existence subject them to the imperatives of practice, tending thereby to prevent the formation and development of the aptitude for symbolic mastery of practice' (p. 48).

What, then, does the development of this 'symbolic mastery in its
most accomplished form' depend on? On the language learnt in early
childhood in the family environment. This language is supposed to be
more or less complex:

> language [. . .] provides, together with a richer or poorer vocabulary,
> a more or less complex system of categories, so that the capacity to
> decipher and manipulate complex structures [. . .] depends partly
> on the complexity of the language transmitted by the family (p. 73).

One can see that there is nothing new in this analysis of linguistic
practices: since Passeron and Bourdieu exclude power relations from it,
they inevitably fall back on the establishment of a hierarchy between
class languages. So the manner in which they criticize Bernstein is
surprising:

> Bernstein tends to reduce to intrinsic characteristics of the language,
> such as degree of syntactic complexity, differences whose unifying,
> generative principle lies in the different types of relation to language,

themselves embedded in different systems of attitudes towards the world and other people (p. 133).

Apart from reiterating the terms of richness and complexity themselves, what do they have to say more than Bernstein, who has ceaselessly emphasized that each class cuts out a different system of meanings according to its conditions of existence?

They think they have found something new which enables them to avoid reification, an explicative principle: 'relation to language': 'So it is in the relation to language that one finds the principle underlying the most visible differences between bourgeois language and working-class language' (p. 116). But they always valorize only one type of relation to language:

> The opposition between these two types of relation to language stems from the opposition between the two modes of acquiring verbal mastery, the exclusively scholastic acquisition which condemns the acquirer to a 'scholastic' relation to scholastic language and the mode of acquisition through insensible familiarization, which alone can fully produce the practical mastery of language and culture . . . (p. 119).

The dominated classes' relationship to language, a language which is immersed in concrete situations, is meant to be a mere product of 'the vital urgencies which thrust a pragmatic disposition on the dominated classes' (p. 49). In short, the language of the dominated would be no more than a mere verbal scansion of their deeds and behaviour. Since the authors fail to see that language is a component of a class identity which is fundamentally defined by dominance relationships imposing the use of 'je' (I) here, and the use of 'on' (one) there, and thus fail to see the ideological dimension of linguistic practices, once again the dominated are attributed the status of objects.

However, and this is a graver scientific error, the dominated exist in the analyses of the authors of *Reproduction* no more than on an abstract level, an error which for his part Bernstein did not make, since in his research practice he gave dominated language as much attention as dominant language. On the contrary, there is nothing here on the language of the dominated. All the attention is focused on the productions of the dominant class; since it is valued as more complex, it is considered in all its complexity. One is invited to take note of the nuances in meaning between the attitudes of grammarians, scholastic rhetoricians and avant-garde or rear-guard writers. Class ethnocentricity then becomes caste ethnocentricity through selective attention to an intellectual fraction of the dominant class. However, what can we learn from the discourse on class languages in which the practices of the dominated are not considered?

As real participants, language professionals are supposed to have the power to act on language by creating a system of differences. They would constantly seek to distinguish themselves through rare productions which the others would desperately attempt to imitate. One returns to a banal explanation of the voluntarist type, even if disguised as pseudo-materialist discourse. Indeed, the authors tell us of 'the extreme form of the literary disposition towards language which is proper to the privileged classes, who are inclined to make the choice of language and the manner of its use a means of excluding the vulgar and thereby affirming their distinction' (p. 118). In a more recent article, 'Le fétichisme de la langue',[8] Bourdieu develops the idea that this wish for distinction would be an efficient principle of transformation:

> The linguistic field owes its original dynamics to a particular form of class struggle which is spelled out in the very structure of the field, and which continually opposes pretension and distinction, the withholders and the pretenders, the aristocrats and the bourgeois.

As we have seen in Chapter 3, the dominant class does not choose specific forms merely to distinguish itself. If it uses certain signifiers and a certain syntactic order, it is because they are suited to the expression and strengthening of its effectiveness over the world and over mankind. On the other hand, referring to the history of facts of language allows a relativization of the idea that a social group has the power to orient language. Symbolic crystallization of the specific power relationships at any given time, the discourses produced by both one and the other class regulate the transformation of the structure of the oppositions between class languages. The relationship to language is no more than a power relationship which is uttered, either by the power submitted to or the power wielded. If one analyses class languages while trying to grasp the meaning of their oppositions, one notices that essentialist ideology determines the contents and forms of all discourse and that as an instrument of domination it is all the more effective because it is acted out by the social agents themselves.

To talk of unequally distributed goods, of a different disposition towards language, of the economic or psychological value of a bargainable possession, presupposes an analysis of the facts of language with reference to one group, the group which possesses, as well as the economic power, the power to impose its world view. And in the dynamic of transformation, the motor role is yet again attributed to the dominant group.

A certain kind of 'fixism'
As they centred their studies exclusively on the production of the

dominant and attributed them a superiority in logical mastery, consequently forgetting to analyse the social relationships between the classes, Bourdieu and Passeron tend to suggest a fixist view of social reality. It all seems as though the 'lack' of linguistic capital has been substituted for the 'lack' of aptitudes, with the same distortion for sociological analysis: nobody can escape the consequences of linguistic deprivation from early education on.

The chosen few According to the authors, the chances of ascent by means of school are predetermined in accordance with linguistic capital and class ethos: '. . . the educational process of differential elimination according to social class [. . .] is the product of the continuous action of the factors which define the positions of the different classes with regard to the school system, i.e. *cultural capital* and *class ethos*' (p. 87). But their discourse becomes confused when they try to explain the presence of a small minority of children of the working classes at university. By excluding all recourse to other explicative factors from the outset so as to give preference only to cultural factors, the authors are forced to use arguments of a psychological nature: supposedly these children show 'ability to turn a first-rate pupil's docile doggedness into academic ease by dint of doggedness and docility . . .' (p. 201).[9]

The problem seems to them to be different as regards the 'middle classes', who also have few advantages in their favour, but who 'self-eliminate' themselves less often than children from the working classes. Indeed, the authors suppose from the results of the test that middle-class children have the lowest pedagogic message reception level.[10] At this point their arguments adopt a dominant scheme which associates mass = drop in level, and conversely, over-selection = élite:

Analysis of the variations over time of the relative weight of the categories of receivers thus enables one to detect and explain sociologically a tendency towards a continuous fall in the *mode* of distribution of the receivers' linguistic competences, together with an increased *dispersion* of this distribution. Owing to the increased rate of enrolment of all social classes, the corrective effect of over-selection acts less and less on the reception level of the categories with the weakest linguistic heritage (as can already be seen in the case of students of middle-class origin) . . . (p. 91).

In short, if we understand it correctly, the growth in students has been accompanied by a drop in level, but all the classes are not responsible to the same extent. The categories which seem worthy of consideration due to their level would appear to be, on the one hand, students from the dominant class who have been able to draw profit from their cultural capital, and, on the other hand, the small group of working-class children who have succeeded in their social ascent thanks to their 'exceptional qualities' and efforts. The middle classes are supposed to overcrowd universities, since their lack of the required linguistic competence is not compensated for by the merit of over-selection.

Those who wonder about the possibilities of a growth in students from the working classes are warned that:

> It also follows from these analyses that if the proportion of working-class students entering university were significantly increased, those students' degree of relative selection would, as it declined, less and less offset the educational handicaps related to the unequal social-class distribution of linguistic and cultural capital (p. 76).

Doubtless, here the sources of the scientific discourse's incoherency lies in the authors' acceptance of élitist values. Incoherency indeed, for if the statement refers to working-class children as a whole, how can it be affirmed that the more a group is eliminated the more this 'compensates' for 'scholastic disadvantages'? And if the statement refers to each particular individual, does the fact of being over-selected, i.e. of getting very good scholastic results, 'compensate' for a 'scholastic disadvantage'?

Circular relations   Everything is presented as a system which reproduces itself without fault. The authors establish relations of a circular kind between what materialist theory defines as infrastructure and super-structure. Moreover, they tell us that they aim to grasp '. . . the system of circular relations which unite *structures* and *practices*, through the mediation of habitus, qua products of the structures, producers of practices and reproducers of the structures . . .' (p. 203). Thus, there would be a perfect adequacy between objective structures and habitus, and the reproduction mechanisms would have no defects: 'the objective structures produce class habitus and in particular the dispositions and predispositions which, in generating practices adapted to these structures, enable the structures to function and be perpetuated . . .' (p. 204).

In fact, one is confronted with a fragmentation of social reality and not with an attempt to establish dialectic relations between instances of social reality. The discourse of *Reproduction* is based on a constant dichotomy: physical violence/symbolic violence; power relations/ meaning relations; material conditions/linguistic capital; exteriority/ interiority; objective/subjective. Of course, a scientific study cannot avoid an analytic division of reality, but why content oneself with always positing two heterogeneous realities, two poles, with the aim of establishing relations between them? To be sure, the authors' ambition lies elsewhere, but if they wish to contribute to the development of knowledge in the social sciences by renouncing a causal, linear pattern of thought favouring one of the poles, whether objective or subjective, can they be content to write: 'objective regularities are internalized in the form of subjective expectations [. . .] the latter are expressed in objective behaviours which contribute towards the realization of objective probabilities' (p. 173)?

Perhaps it would be necessary in the first place to examine at least the coexisting relations between the objective dimension of behaviour (who enrolls or does not enroll at university? Who works while pursuing their studies? Who attends the courses? Who takes the exams?) and the subjective dimension (what does each social agent have to say about his scholastic choices, about his social group's possibilities and about those of the others?). In this way, they could see that social agents do not necessarily passively conform to objective determinisms.[11] Dominant discourse, source of the fragmentation of the identity of the dominated, of the formal 'incoherence' of their utterances and of the discontinuity in their behaviour, is for them at the same time the basis of their impulse to question dominance relations. On the side of non-power, the relationship to language is generally silence; not only is speech not perceived as capable of changing concrete reality, but, furthermore, words can only be suspect since the dominant have turned them into a tool for domination. Therefore, for the dominated, self-awareness as a future identity (and no longer as an identity defined once and for all) leads to a questioning of the most banal language, with detailed attention to the meaning of a social discourse which encases them in the idea of their specificity, of the immutability of their domination.

Failing to proceed to a dialectical analysis, failing to give themselves the means by which to reveal at least the concomitant relations between exteriority and interiority, the authors are reduced to asking themselves metaphysical questions which are sociologically devoid of meaning: 'We leave it to others to decide whether the relations between power relations and sense relations are, in the last analysis, sense relations or power relations' (p. 15). This is certainly a dominant person's question which is never raised by those who experience these relations as a single reality and not as two separate orders. Power relations and sense relations are homogeneous realities, except that they obey different processes.

Inattentiveness?   Passeron and Bourdieu are continuously demystifying essentialist ideology present in commonsense statements; their efforts to take their distances from this ideology are real, but they only know it in its explicit form as an explanation of social success through natural gifts. Nevertheless, one can consider their questioning of the theory of natural aptitudes as incomplete, since they do not refrain from using extremely ideologized concepts: by constantly using such apparently banal words as 'aptitude', 'disposition', 'predisposition', etc., without

137

their knowing it their discourse constitutes a form of dominant 'cultural arbitrary'. The ideological impact of these words is irrefutable whatever meaning they themselves wish to give them.

Repressed essentialist ideology reveals itself precisely in the liberties which a discourse otherwise attempting to be rigorous allows itself, in the laxness with which certain notions are defined, in unguarded lapses into the spontaneity of a metaphor or an analogy. Thus the dominant ideology's scheme of reality perception suddenly brings the authors to use an analogy of the biological kind completely inappropriate with the book's rationally developed theory: 'Education [. . .] is the equivalent, in the cultural order, of the transmission of genetic capital in the biological order. If the habitus is the analogue of genetic capital, then the inculcation [. . .] is the analogue of generation . . .' (p. 32). The same scheme, so strongly anchored in the unconscious of all the agents involved in a class system, impairs reasoning in an until then perfectly logical sequence: to assert 'the "value" of an occupation (such as, in France, that of primary or secondary school teacher) steadily diminishes as it is feminized' (p. 183), implies that an occupation's value is destroyed – in the economic and psychological senses – by an alleged 'feminine nature'. The authors suddenly forget what sociological studies have clarified: when a professional sector becomes less profitable economically, the active male population abandons it to the economically exploited sex class as well shown by E. Sullerot.[12]

Of course, it should be reaffirmed that there is no question of an explicit fixist stand-point. The authors' theory is diametrically opposite to those which pretend to explain the facts of scholastic selection by the 'nature of things'. But it is important to disclose the ever-lively presence, in a critical scientific discourse, of an essentialist ideology with which all researchers in the social sciences are confronted in their daily practice. Passeron and Bourdieu are also subject to the thought patterns of the overall culture; the conceptual tools they forged for themselves are, in the eyes of the reader, handled as beings and not as functions, and they end up by expressing the idea of fixity and irreversibility.

Proof for this was provided in 1968. At a time when 'class university' was violently questioned, debates on 'democratization' drew their arguments from the thesis which alleged itself to be radically opposite to the theory of natural aptitudes. Analysis of the contents of debates held at the time in student assemblies,[13] analysis of various proposals for educational reforms and of articles in the major newspapers, all testify to the new explicative theory's success from that time on. Thereafter there existed but one creed: it is linguistic and cultural differences, and not differences in aptitudes, which allow us to understand why university is a 'class university' (as we have seen in Chapter 2). A comforting theory for those wishing to hang on to the possession of knowledge, since for them it is once again a question of immutable reality.

If the thesis which replaces aptitudes by the 'unequal repartition of linguistic capital' met with such widespread response, it is due to the fact that the authors' implicit discourse fell back on the evidence of common sense which dominant ideology imposes. Only the way of expressing the message changed, not its real content. Of course, this message was deformed, simplified, but it could be accepted as evidence of common sense only because it contained the germs of a fixist theory. Everything is reproduced . . . including ideological structure, to which scholarly discourse brings its scientific caution.

Notes

1   P. Naville, *Théorie de l'orientation professionnelle*, Paris, Gallimard, 1945.

2   Moreover, it would be important for sociology of knowledge to reveal why a reformulation of the question was possible: the field of theoretical knowledge in France, the structure of the educational and research systems, the social origin of researchers in the social sciences, etc.

3   P. Bourdieu and J. C. Passeron, *Reproduction in Education, Society and Culture*, trans. R. Nice, London and Beverly Hills, Sage Publications, 1977 (French edition 1970). P. Bourdieu and J. C. Passeron, *Rapport pédagogique et communication*, Cahiers du Centre de Sociologie Européenne, Paris, Mouton, 1965, their first analysis of 'cultural heritage'.

4   C. Baudelot and R. Establet, *L'Ecole capitaliste en France*, Paris, Maspero, 1971. V. Petit criticized the fact that the authors tend to assimilate ideology and knowledge in 'Les contradictions de la Reproduction', *La Pensée*, vol. 168, 1973, pp. 3—20.

5   However, the influence of purely economic determinisms had been brought to the fore in the following article: N. Bisseret, 'La sélection universitaire et sa signification pour l'étude des rapports de dominance', *Revue française de sociologie*, vol. 9, no. 4, 1968.

6   The way in which the authors distributed categories of students along this so-called 'linguistic competence' scale, however, leaves one puzzled: a category in which 67 per cent of the students obtained a mark above 12 is labelled (++), hence of a very good level (sons of the upper classes, p. 81, tables 4—5); but another category in which 91 per cent of the students obtained a mark above 12 is in turn labelled (+), hence a good level (sons of the working classes studying in Paris, p. 74, table 1 and p. 75, table 2).

7   The authors would appear not to ignore the fact, since on page 96 they republished (cf. article in note 5) the percentages of boys who took up different disciplines in *Lettres*, in 1963.

8 *Actes de la recherche en sciences sociales*, vol. 4, 1975. He advocates a materialistic analysis of symbolic exchanges, but in his analysis he ignores the material basis of symbolic dominance relations to such an extent that he ends up by making statements of the purest idealism. For example, his ideas on the relationship between dominant language and dominated language in a situation of colonial conflict lead one to suppose that he accords language a causal role in the upset of power relationships: 'The access of an up till then dominated language to the status of *official language* [. . .], of course, has the effect of legitimizing the fact that the possessors of this language appropriate positions of power [. . .] thereby excluding those who owed their dominant position to other linguistic competences.' One can question the idea that those who had to give up political power at the time of colonial independence 'owed their dominant position to other linguistic competences'. One might think that the counter-power which the colonized installed was legitimized long before the change in official language (which is, it seems, a consequence and not an 'effect' of the colonized seizing power).

In a more recent article, 'L'économie des échanges symboliques', *Langue française*, May 1977, Bourdieu returns to the thesis of the differential profitability of linguistic capital and defines the oppositions between the languages of the social classes in terms of their semantic and stylistic aspects, thereby rejecting power relations to an extra-linguistic sphere.

9 Here and there, one learns that they were supposed to have benefited from 'a particularity of their family background', from 'compensatory characteristics' such as an elevated level of instruction on the mother's side, or the grandfather's occupation (p. 104). Surely, they should have examined the marginal position which these families occupy within the dominated class (as we have seen in Chapter 2), since this class is characterized precisely by the absence of any so-called compensatory characteristics.

10 In fact, students from the so-called middle classes get a degree just as often as those from the dominant class (viz. *Les Inégaux ou la sélection universitaire*, Paris, PUF, 1974). Like middle-class children, industrialists' *sons* are meant to be insufficiently selected: 'it can be seen that as this category advances towards quasi-total enrolment, it tends to acquire all the characteristics, in particular the competences and attitudes, associated with the academic under-selection of a category' (p. 93).

11 According to J. Duchatel, in so far as the authors only consider the ideological instance, their analysis cannot satisfy the Marxist definition of social change (since ideology is only meaningful when it is articulated with the class struggle through which the effects of structures are in a relationship of generalized contradiction). Bourdieu and Passeron are content, according to Duchatel, with a functionalistic definition of change (disfunctioning and re-

equilibration, or a factor of modernization). J. Duchatel, *Sociologie et sociétés*, 1971, pp. 103–15.

12 E. Sullerot, *Histoire et sociologie du travail féminin*, Paris, Gonthier, 1968.

13 N. Bisseret, 'Enseignement inégalitaire et contestation étudiante', *Communications*, vol. 12, 1968, pp. 54–65.

Conclusion

Why is it fundamentally important that the social sciences investigate the dissimilarity between class languages? Because we are talking of social practices which are an efficient and necessary part of the dynamics of the social relations of dominance. In order to analyse the dynamic processes, it is not enough to study the power relations in their material dimension, they must also be studied in their ideological dimension, i.e. the manner in which the dominant and the dominated consciously and unconsciously see the appropriation by a small social group of the means of subsistence.

For the study of ideology, language constitutes a privileged means of approach, since it is far from a neutral tool, as can be shown by analysing the transformations in word meaning and syntax. These transformations, as well as the different social usages, have something to do with the social organization of the referent and the dominant ideology of a society. We have seen that when the feudal society of France was transformed into a trading society, when economic power came into the hands of the bourgeoisie, the social referent changed: there was a transference of power from one social group — the nobility, ideologically defined as a collectivity whose practices incarnated the will of a transcendent object, God — to another social group, the bourgeoisie, defined as a sum of individual wills acting on their own accord over the world and over men. At the same time as this bourgeoisie acted, it saw its practices as issuing from a free and creative subject, and it invented a new way of using words: the stress was displaced from the action to the doer of the action; the uttering subject, the 'I', became the centre around which, with the help of possessives and demonstratives, things and human beings were hierarchically ordered. By establishing its social 'order', the bourgeoisie progressively transmuted its own practices, including its verbal practices, into biologically based ontological attributes. This essentialist ideology still imposes on every social participant his/her discursive practices, as can be seen by the topical and morphosyntactical analysis of the discourses of dominated and dominant groups.

142

It is in so far as they themselves are involved in dominance relations that researchers in the social sciences are led to interpret linguistic data as signs of differential aptitudes. It is true that this metaphysical postulate of an isomorphism between language, thought, and anatomo-physical structure, which guided research at the beginning of the century, was later vigorously denounced. From the 1960s on, a critical current made the hypothesis that power relations have something to do with the modalities in verbalizing concrete experiences.

But this stage of intuition has not yet been surpassed, since the approach to class languages is still a mechanistic one: one set of material conditions would in themselves determine a given set of language practices. This dualism, the sign of an idealistic view (even though some researchers think they have a materialistic view), inevitably leads to seeing language as an object in itself. Thus the analysts of the linguistic 'differences' have not been able to avoid the pitfalls of essentialist ideology, which attributes a surplus of 'being' to the dominant, since they define the question in terms of degrees in richness and logical complexity.

We do not pretend to have accomplished here more than proposing some research hypotheses based on an analysis of recorded forms of 'popular' language. But this analysis does show how one could stop treating language practices as if they existed in themselves, independent of the way in which they relate to one another and to the social organization of the referent. Concrete and symbolic domination is one and the same thing; power relations also exist in and through the most ordinary and everyday utterances. They do not exist before language and do not exist without language. This kind of approach breaks with the notion that a language is a neutral tool, independent of dominance relations. That linguistic unification exists does not mean that linguistic homogeneity exists, and one should give up the idea that there is a reality, 'language', considered as a factor of internal cohesion despite social conflicts. Of course one can speak of cohesion, of communication between the dominant and dominated: they can communicate with each other because their speech relates to the same referent.

It is because they fail to recognize this that specialists in the scientific enquiry on class languages have not managed to avoid the trap of prevailing ideology according to which the dominant class sets up its own language habits as an absolute standard. Power relations operate within speech itself, they give meaning to the forms present as well as to those absent in each 'code' and define the system of their oppositions. Oppositions are a necessary, if not sufficient, condition to maintain the social hierarchy, for the forms used by one and the other have something to do with their concrete conditions of existence, inasmuch as they are symbolized, 'explained', by the dominant group. It is the order of the world as acted and uttered by the dominant class that defines the social identity of the dominant ('person', 'subject') and of the dominated ('object'). Dominant speech, in fact, forces the dominated to express themselves in a certain key by means of signifiers which unconsciously have the same *historical* significance for all. In terms of the dominant ideology, to be 'that' (woman, worker, black, Jew, etc.) cannot be good, whatever one feels. For all, it is 'bad' to be non-power, it means that one is a species apart.

One should certainly analyse the language practices of the categories whose age, sex, colour of skin, etc., assign them a special place in the social relations of production, and include the question of language and social classes in the more general problem of language and dominance relations. It seems as if the concrete and verbal practices of power impose an identity on dominated categories which induces them to adopt specific language practices, but not arbitrarily. For example, they almost inevitably announce the category to which they belong. Certain practices common to all dominated show that they both reject and submit to power: the working classes' 'coarse' language, women's 'frivolous' language, schoolchildren's 'slang' are ways of taking refuge and attempts to assert oneself which, at the same time, lock one in the definition imposed by the dominant.

Socially rejected 'elsewhere', the dominated, in order to avoid the annihilation of their 'me', have no other option but to identify *individually* with the hidden referent of the social discourse. A black man can dream himself a-white-chased-by-a-mean-black, and a woman can be a misogynist, only because in their unconscious both of them are not only an element of a social category but a power which says 'I'. This shows the effectiveness of dominant discourse which structures the psyche of the dominated in such a way that there is a necessary heterogeneity between their imaginary 'I' and their social 'me' (set of practices of an oppressed and devaluated being). The 'I' and the 'me' can be homogeneous ('ego') only for the dominant.

We have seen that the group in possession of the means of subsistence states the coherence of the universe, of his universe ('I am'). The others state the split in that universe. What could they articulate other than what for them is necessarily the incoherence of the universe? Are they 'object' or 'subject'? Who is 'who' and who is 'what'? The language practices of the dominated can only express and strengthen the fragmentation of their 'ego', as long as social identity is essentialized. Therefore, silence is often the language of non-power, the only possible way when the contradictions are insurmountable; concrete violence is the only language to signify the refusal of concrete and ideological domination.

This type of approach enables one to question the studies which assimilate formal coherence to discursive coherence. The way in which the dominant define themselves cannot be contradictory, but for the dominated things are more complicated since the dominant practices situate them at the heart of contradiction. All speakers try to introduce a logical sequence in their utterances so as to escape the simultaneity of the contradictions experienced. Even if one can pick out inconsistencies in their speech (the scientific discourse on natural aptitudes is formally coherent which does not exclude it from having logical contradictions), only speakers of the dominant class resolve the contradictions by introducing into their speech logical operators which restore a formal coherence among their utterances.

One can therefore ask oneself if the use of signifiers such as conjunctions does not point to a form of censorship, whereby the dominant assure themselves of a logical order which masks the contradictions in their speech. They thereby reassure themselves through their own knowledge and their language and this allows them to deny the others power owing to their so-called 'incapacity' shown by the 'incoherence' of their speech. It seems as if, by means of the signs of reason and logic which they use to give formal coherence to their discourse on life, the dominant try to ward off the idea of relativity of their power, of the historicity of their social order.